Kitchenalia

Kitchenalia

Furnishing and Equipping your Kitchen with Flea Market Finds and Period Pieces

Vinny Lee

jacqui
small

First published in 2014 by
Jacqui Small LLP
An imprint of Aurum Books
74–77 White Lion Street
London N1 9PF

Publisher: Jacqui Small
Senior Commissioning Editor: Fritha Saunders
Managing Editor: Lydia Halliday
Designer: Penny Stock
Editor: Sian Parkhouse
Production: Maeve Healy
Special photography: Darren Chung

2016 2015 2014

10 9 8 7 6 5 4 3 2 1

Printed in China

To AWJ – an invaluable piece of Kitchenalia

ISBN 978 1 909342 49 1

A catalogue record for this book is
available from the British Library.

Contents

Kitchenalia is the stuff with which you furnish and kit out your kitchen – the jugs and jars, pots and pans, bowls and baskets. It is all the things you acquire and accumulate to make your kitchen a useful and enjoyable place to be.

ABOVE A poaching pan on a retro-styled cooker.

RIGHT 1950s English Rose units with a melamine-topped table and chairs from the same era.

Some of these things may be new but most will be sourced from a vintage or classic design base. Almost everything I prepare or cook in my kitchen involves a little bit of history and often a memory. There is a favourite old serving spoon with a monogrammed handle that I use for stirring sugar into a meringue or flour into a sponge cake mix. The spoon reminds me of my childhood and baking with my mother, because she used the same spoon.

There are weighing scales that belonged to my grandmother and plates and bowls from my mother-in-law and grandmother-in-law. Often they are referred to by name or house name, such as Granny Hunter's plate or the Rockmount bowl, because they are remembered by their association with that person or place.

These things may be old, but they are still useful, with a patina of age and a familiarity that makes them special. They are objects that have survived because they perform the function for which they were made and have withstood the test of time, sometimes in the hands of several generations.

I also have a collection of blue-and-white plates found in second-hand shops and markets while on holiday, so they have memories of the time and place where they were found, whether it was a sunny weekend in Saltburn-by-the-Sea or a damp day out in Hastings. Then there are things given to me as presents by friends who share an interest in cooking or know my weakness for a certain style of china or type of gadget.

Kitchenalia can be a collection of hand-me-downs and presents, some with a specific purpose, others just because you like them. It can be made up of things that are useful, beautiful or often both; you have them in your home because you enjoy using them and having them around you gives you daily pleasure.

Sourcing — Modern & Vintage

Vintage objects come from many places. Some may be inherited, others given as gifts, or, for the ardent collector, it may be a question of sifting through on-line sale sites, auction houses, second-hand shops, car boot and garage sales. Sourcing and collecting Kitchenalia can become addictive; you will find yourself constantly on the look-out.

A number of manufacturers have been looking back through their archives to find 'new' ideas, having realized that an early or original style they once produced still has appeal. They then create a technically updated version, but with the same styling and intrinsic appeal of the old. And times and food fashions change – some years ago the food processor was the all-singing, all-dancing gadget, but now more and more retro-style food mixers and blenders are to be found in kitchens. The modern flat-fronted, steel-clad fridge-freezer and ice-maker used to be the must-have appliance; nowadays, the rounded and often coloured 1950s look is making a comeback.

Many designers, such as Cath Kidston and Orla Kiely, take inspiration from the past for their kitchenware designs. Kidston's nostalgic prints of roses, strawberries and polka dots in pastel

ABOVE A mid-century poster, red melamine and jaunty red-and-white gingham contribute to the American diner feel.

RIGHT A pine table, metal chairs and cooker create a utilitarian feel, softened by the blind and plates display.

THIS PAGE Open shelves and painted wood give a soft, country-style look to a small kitchen where tableware and storage are both on display and on hand to use.

colours with a splash of primary have a reassuring sweetness about them, while Kiely has a more modern vintage look, with strong mid-century Scandinavian overtones. Her embossed ceramic storage jars, tiered cake stand and nests of cake tins would look as at home in a 1950s kitchen as a contemporary one.

When buying vintage pieces check that they are still in good condition. Cracked china is fine for display but shouldn't be used to eat or serve from, because it might be unhygienic. And don't be tempted to give it a thorough wash in a dishwasher as this could cause the cracks to open up and the dish to break. If you are buying pre-used electric gadgets and equipment they will need to be checked by a professional, and possible rewired to comply with current safety standards. Sometimes you can keep the outside shell of the old appliance, but put a new machine or engine inside.

When sourcing vintage objects, whether on on-line auctions sites, through specialist shops or car boots sales, you need to be specific in your purchases. There is a temptation to buy something just because it looks good, but you have to ask yourself questions. Does it work? Secondly, is it compatible with things I already have? If I have one already, is this in better condition and could it be a replacement, or will it just add to the pile in the drawer or cupboard?

The *Kitchenalia* kitchen will inevitably be a mix of old and new, usually new units and electrical goods with vintage wares and china. To blend the two successfully, try to base your look on a colour or theme, or around a collection, and find a fit between the kitchen style and your collection. For example, Midwinter Queensberry's 1960s Midwinter china range has a crisp stripe pattern in black, white and olive green, which sits comfortably in a modern, pared-down kitchen, whereas more ornate floral china such as Royal Albert will appear over-fussy and colourful.

ABOVE You might be lucky enough to have inherited a complete dinner service, like this pretty off-white set, or have found one to buy. If you are not so fortunate, you can still build up a set gradually from mismatched pieces, adding to it as you make new discoveries.

RIGHT Antique storage jars may be chipped or cracked and therefore unusable for their original purpose, but can still be a decorative feature on a dresser or shelf.

OPPOSITE, CLOCKWISE FROM TOP LEFT A mid-century vintage Lotus design covered casserole manufactured by the Norwegian company Cathrineholm.

Painted wooden-handled utensils hang from butcher's hooks suspended from an equally colourful old enamelled advertising sign.

Many manufacturers create new machines with retro styling so that they incorporate modern technology, but have the look of another era.

Copper conducts heat quickly and efficiently and is often used for pots and pans in professional kitchens.

LEFT Oblong Metro tiles and caged, bulkhead lights give a practical and utilitarian edge to this simply styled kitchen.

ABOVE An old aluminium colander can be used for more than straining and washing vegetables – it may also have a life as a container.

THIS PAGE A classically styled kitchen like this may feature a number of collections, such as storage jars, coffee pots, sugar bowls and jugs, but they all sit comfortably together because they are in compatible shades of white or off-white.

TEA   SUGAR   FLOUR

FLOUR

Four ways to transform a kitchen

To show how much impact accessories and colour have on a room, and how dramatically they can change the look, we asked three inspirational design teams to dress the same classic, country-house-style kitchen.

The kitchen has many features, such as Georgian-inspired panelled doors, a freestanding cook's table, a separate china cupboard and a plate rack over the double ceramic sink. The results, found on the following pages, show clearly that each one is highly individual and packed with interest and impact. The differences are not only in choices of colour and pattern, but also in the objects selected and how and where they are displayed. Some chose to make the area over the oven a focus, while others wallpapered the back of the china cupboard and made that an area of interest. There were those who decided to balance the impact of pattern with plain white china and clear glass, while others ramped up the intensity by mixing contrasting patterns and bold colours.

White on white

This well-appointed room provides a clean and timeless backdrop that can be simply accessorized with plain white china or decorated in a variety of ways.

One-colour pattern

Then we went to East London style queen Frieda Gormley, of the luxury British interiors, fashion and lifestyle brand House of Hackney, and suggested that she bring what is usually regarded as her 'boudoir' style to a daytime kitchen setting.

Eclectic & colourful

The first designers are June Summerill and Bernadette Bishop of Summerill & Bishop. We asked them to give the kitchen a makeover that would bring together the elegant and eclectic mix of modern, vintage and global for which their shop is known (see opposite also).

Mixed pattern & tonal colour palette

Lastly we approached Keith Stephenson and Mark Hampshire of Mini Moderns, known for their outstanding use of pattern and colour, to transform the kitchen with their 1950s-inspired graphic designs, china, wallpapers and range of recycled paints.

White on white

Although we refer to this kitchen as a white kitchen, it isn't in fact white. The English kitchen by Martin Moore & Company, used as the base for our styling experiment, has a subtle off-white finish and the floor is covered in a dense Purbeck stone, called 'Aged Farringdon', which has mottled beige to tan colouring with interesting fossil markings. There is also a stainless-steel splashback behind the oven. As well as giving protection and reflecting light it provides a contemporary edge that prevents the look from becoming too much of a period piece.

If the room had been decorated with nothing but bright white it would have had a very clinical and hard appearance, verging on the institutional and lacking any feeling of warmth and comfort. But because the colours used are warmer 'shades of white' there is a welcoming feel to the room. The scheme is simple – there are no contrasting colours or patterns to distract the eye, and so the finishes and details become more important. Your eye is drawn to the panelling of the doors and the shapely pillars that divide and support the various sections. Furnishings and finishes, such as the woven basketwork of the counter stools, the 'Joe' design by Vincent Sheppard, stand out, as do the vintage-style, ribbed-glass light shades over the cook's table, from BTC Lighting's Prismatic range.

The French farmhouse double-bowl ceramic sink is located beneath a useful plate rack and the white Lacanche Macon oven, with four burners and simmer plates, surrounded by the stainless-steel splashback, has a traditional appearance that sits comfortably with the traditional styling of the furniture while remaining a wholly twenty-first-century machine.

This English kitchen comes from the family-owned and run business Martin Moore & Company, founded in 1975. The managing director and founder Barbara Moore has this style of kitchen in her own home and describes why it suits her part medieval cottage in North Yorkshire. 'The design combines fitted and freestanding elements, both of which can be scaled up or down. It is adaptable and works in any period building, from rural cottage to period town house,' she says. For this opening scheme, showcasing the neutral canvas the designers were given to work with, the kitchen has been styled to look simple and understated. 'I especially like the look you get from mixing lots of

different pieces of white china together; some is classic French style with scalloped edges while other pieces are contemporary with a textured, raised surface. But because they are all white they can be mixed and matched,' says Barbara.

The concept of this style of kitchen is to give the pieces the look of freestanding furniture rather than the standard streamlined and fitted units. For example, the sink area is set forward as a separate piece, with columns at each side, and the wall cupboards are arranged symmetrically above the base furniture to achieve the appearance of a dresser.

ABOVE Modern but retro-styled weighing scales and food mixer sit alongside the mix of white and off-white china.

RIGHT Displayed china and glassware can be a decorative feature and turn basic storage into a focal point of the room.

Eclectic & colourful

We start with a gentle build-up of spot colour and a mix of wares from around the world. This look is put together by longtime friends June Summerill and Bernadette Bishop, who share a passion for cooking and spend a lot of time in their kitchens. In 1994 they created a kitchen shop selling only the things they liked and would have in their own home, a mix of old and new, beautiful and practical utensils, cookware, ceramics, glass, vintage linens, candles, household brushes, which they source from France, Italy, Belgium, England, South Africa, Germany and the Middle East. The history and character that comes with vintage pieces is off set by the new, such as the coloured Clair Glassware that they have specially made by a French artisan and has the glassblower's signature on the bottom of each piece. They chose this glassware as part of their scheme to introduce 'spot' colour to the plain kitchen.

Among the classic objects and utensils are the Peugeot Paris salt and pepper mills made by the company whose trademark lion symbol has been in use from around the time it produced its first coffee grinder in 1840. There are also batteries of traditional knives from manufacturers Nontron and Opinel. The Nontron knife, with its traditional boxwood handle, has been manufactured in the village of Nontron, in the Dordogne area of southern France, since the fifteenth century. The handle is usually decorated with pokerwork designs based on a distinctive logo, and the knives are now highly prized as a style item. Then there is the Opinel knife, created by Joseph Opinel in 1890 in the Savoie region where it was used by the local farmers, herdsmen and *paysans-vignerons* (peasant winemakers). The company is still run by the Opinel family, and sells around 15 million knives each year.

Other pieces used in the scheme are Wonki Ware plates and dishes from the Di Marshall Pottery in South Africa; these are wonderfully uneven with a handmade look and perfectly suit an informal style of entertaining. Substantial pestle and mortars for grinding spices and herbs, with large but light cork platters all add to the interest and variety of the Summerill & Bishop kitchen.

ABOVE RIGHT There are water-washed Italian linens, vintage green glass storage jars and brushes for cleaning inside spouts and bottles among the rich mix of old and new.

RIGHT Texture is an important part of the scheme. These beaten tin-plated copper cooking pots are from Syria. Classic knives and salt and pepper pots are also to hand.

FAR RIGHT 'I can't envisage a house without some vintage pieces, they give a place authenticity,' says Bernadette Bishop.

One-colour pattern

From the white kitchen with spot colour we progress to the same kitchen dressed with a quantity of a single colour, in this case green, and added pattern, a palm leaf motif. This scheme was put together by Frieda Gormley and her husband Javvy M Royle, the founders and directors of House of Hackney.

The company they formed in 2010 began as an interiors label with the mission of 'taking the beige out of interiors'. There is a strong emphasis on quality and design with the aim of having all their wares made in England. The House of Hackney collection of prints and products have a strong Victorian heritage, but with a modern spin. 'We reference traditional crafts and artisan skills but adapt and rework them for a new generation,' says Frieda. The main, and immediate, impact is made by their liberal use of the Palmeral wallpaper in off-white and green, which covers all available wall surfaces. In the

area behind the sink and where water or fat may be splashed the paper can be covered by a panel of plain reinforced glass, for protection, without diminishing its effect.

The Palmeral pattern was inspired by a grand palm house built in Hackney in 1842 by George Loddige as part of his Hackney Botanic Nursery. His palm house, built using the latest curvilinear iron glazing boards and central heating systems, was known as the world's largest. His invention of a system of warm mist-like rain kept the tropical palms, orchids, ferns and camellias in 'rainforest' conditions and enabled him to grow many new species of tropical plant for the first time in Europe.

'The Palm House was a global phenomenon and pre-dated Kew Gardens, where building only started in 1844. Sadly Loddige's Palm House was demolished in the 1950s, but

we were inspired by the history of this amazing building,' says Javvy. 'He was very progressive for the time and Hackney was a different place back then,' adds Frieda.

The Palmeral wallpaper comes with the more 'boudoir' backgrounds of midnight blue or black, but for the kitchen Frieda selected the print on a bright-white background. She also heightened the impact of the print by adding the same pattern on china and linens, but then kept the balance by diluting them with classic plain white china and transparent glassware, so that the whole scheme is balanced.

The plant motif and bright green of the print give the kitchen a fresh and zesty appearance, making it the sort of room that is inviting and invigorating on even the darkest and dreary mornings. Because of the scale of the pattern it might become claustrophobic if used to such an extent in a smaller kitchen, so instead you could choose to use it on a feature wall and allow the printed linens and china to carry the theme through. And in a kitchen where the units are faced with wood or laminate wood-effect doors the 'forest' aspect of the leafy design may become exaggerated and overpowering, so it might be worth looking to other wallpaper prints that would work with a brown, wood element.

FAR LEFT Adding linens with the same pattern but a black background gives the scheme another layer without introducing other colours or patterns.

LEFT Mixing patterned china with plain white and glassware helps to balance the arrangement in this china cabinet.

ABOVE The wallpaper makes a strong impact on the room, but it is diluted and diffused by the single colour and classic style of the units.

Mixed pattern & tonal colour palette

We've seen the impact of a single colour and solo pattern but when Keith Stephenson and Mark Hampshire of Mini Moderns took on the task of decorating the plain kitchen they focused on colour and multiple patterns. 'We used our Darjeeling wallpaper because it has a tiled look, making it instantly appropriate to the kitchen. We offset the freshness of this tessellated design with our rich 1970s-style Paisley Crescent wallpaper, used in the china cupboard and area above the stove. Then we added areas of plain blue Lido paint from our Environmentally Responsible Paints range. The pattern of the vintage Midwinter Cherry Tree china in the plate rack and cupboard combines the turquoise colour with olive and orange, so we brought together some new and old pieces that tied in with those colours, then added the "Granny Takes a Trip" framed print for a bit of retro graphic humour,' says Mark.

'We've always been interested in pattern, from clothing, to furnishing and ceramics and have collected vintage or "second-hand stuff" as we called it, for as long as we've been able to buy things. In the 1980s we both wore almost exclusively second-hand clothes; 1950s shirts were a constant source of inspiration. While trawling charity shops to fill our wardrobes, it was hard to resist a few ceramic gems. I built up a full dinner service of Woods Ware Beryl in this way and Mark has always been a car boot fan and is particularly keen on old branded tins, like the French Bouillon Kub tin, found in a Paris flea market,' says Keith.

The pair are still avid vintage seekers. Mark says that a collection often starts with a serendipitous flea market find, but is then completed by eBay searches because they are impatient and on-line is the quickest way to fill in the gaps. Their own kitchen at home also features a mix of old and new pieces. 'Our everyday china is new, robust and replaceable, but our best dinner services, of which we have three used in rotation, are all old. Gadgets tend to be new but with vintage storage jars and tins sprinkled among them,' says Mark, who then goes on to point out his favourite gadget, a Tala Cook's Dry Measure. 'Being more of a cook than a baker I don't tend to measure things very often. I like to call this slap-dash approach "rustic", but when I need to, this makes it so much easier than faffing about with scales.' Keith loves the Cathrineholm teapot. 'Not only is it classic Scandinavian design, but, being metal, it is also very practical. You can set it on top of a wood-burning stove and your tea stays warm!' he says.

This scheme gives the kitchen a brilliant and bright appearance with a subtle 1950s vintage overtone. The light tile-inspired Darjeeling paper could be used in both large and small kitchens, while the darker and more intense Paisley would need to be used with care in a small room. But it makes an effective background against which to display pale or brightly coloured china, as can be seen here in the china cupboard.

BELOW Paisley Crescent wallpaper and Lido blue paint frame the Lacanche Macon oven and stainless-steel splashback.

RIGHT The same wallpaper was used to line the back of the china cabinet and helps to draw attention to the china.

OVERLEAF Tile-like Darjeeling wallpaper covers the main area of wall around the sink, while the inside of the plate rack has been painted with Lido blue.

The Kitchenalia

Kitchen

Kitchenalia kitchens are

more than just rooms in which to prepare and cook food; they are the heart of a home and a place where character and style is important.

ABOVE A simple rail above the stove provides ample hanging space for tools and utensils.

PREVIOUS PAGES Classic chairs, vintage glassware and an oversized clock give this room an interesting appearance.

This particular genre of kitchen brings together vintage and new, family treasures and brilliant finds, given cohesion by a theme or colour palette and a basic decorating knowledge. We showcase seven key categories of Kitchenalia kitchen, and a number are closely connected. In some cases you may find that when planning a scheme for your kitchen you will want to reference or draw on more than one style or look, and that is fine – a little cross-fertilization will help you create your own particular look.

The retro and reclaimed themes have a lot in common, yet each has its own easy-to-follow direction. The retro kitchen draws directly from 1950s modern and mid-century design, the colour and innovations of the time. The reclaimed kitchen takes recycling as its main motif, but this is not just for cost-effectiveness – it is about a love of things that have history, age and patina. The comforting and reassuring appearance of weathered wood and old metal features strongly, as does an emphasis on the quality that many of these old, pre-used materials and furniture possess.

Other categories that have shared links are the white, painted and country kitchens. The white kitchen is a classic, but in this context it is about a lived-in and comfortable space, rather than minimalist style. The painted kitchen uses colour to give character and identity, but may also be employed to freshen and revitalize old or vintage pieces of furniture or units. The country kitchen is primarily about styling and arranging objects and materials that reference the simple, rural way of life, whether from your immediate vicinity or from further aboard.

And then there is the collector's kitchen. Again, this crosses into the other sections in that the country kitchen may have collections of baskets or dairy ware and the Retro a selection of advertising ware, but for the purposes of *Kitchenalia* style this section is about arranging and displaying groups of china, old utensils and objects and things that have been lovingly gathered and cherished. Finally, utilitarian style is perhaps the most pared down and functional of the looks. It features recycling, but focuses more on industrial sources and commercial inspiration. This is a style that can be scaled up or down to fit into the size of your room. It is also a good starter style, because many of the materials can be sourced inexpensively through scrapyards and skips. As your budget increases you can replace and add to make a more filled in and finished space.

THIS PAGE Ornate lighting, a decorative tiled floor and an elegant table and chairs give this kitchen and dining area a refined and sophisticated appearance.

The Retro Kitchen

A vintage or retro-style kitchen has the appearance of coming from another time or era. Although some items might actually be old, others may be new but made in the style of an earlier design. The period of focus for the *Kitchenalia* retro kitchen is the 1950s, although a little of the decade before and the decade after might just sneak in.

Colour is an important part of this style of kitchen. Paint had been in short supply during World War II and the period immediately after, so household colour had been dictated by manufacturers, left-over stock rather than fashionable trends. But by the end of the era bright new colours, such as pink, chartreuse and turquoise joined red, yellow and black as favourites, and graphic design and cartoon-style drawings were widely used in wallpapers and fabrics. New materials such as plastic also had an impact on the style and availability of homeware.

ABOVE LEFT Positioned between two doorways, this wooden cabinet with painted panels is used to store china and tableware.

LEFT The kitchen opens onto an enclosed porch where an Adirondack chair picks up on the country-style theme.

RIGHT A circular mat on the red linoleum floor helps to differentiate the relaxed sitting area from the kitchen and dining zone.

Colourful cabinets

BELOW Sky-blue walls and sunny yellow furniture capture the enthusiasm for colour popular in the post-war period. After years of decorating with a restricted palette the opportunity to brighten up was eagerly embraced.

RIGHT The simple but striking black-and-white chequerboard floor, laid on the diagonal, picks up on geometric designs popular in the 1950s. This type of vinyl or lino tiled floor is hard-wearing and practical.

FAR RIGHT A vintage unit, such as the double-height one shown here, can be stripped, refurbished and painted to match other furniture, such as the melamine-topped table, giving a cohesive and coordinated look.

The retro kitchen is a colourful and fun place to be, and draws inspiration from a period of dramatic change in both social outlook and design, and the kitchen of the 1950s home is probably where the biggest and most notable revolution took place. At the time, advertising for kitchen wares and domestic machines was second only to the latest cars.

A wide range of innovative machines and gadgets started to come on the market, and because they were mostly mass-produced in factories they were cheaper to create and therefore more affordable for many people. Also the new architectural style was to open up rooms, making them lighter, brighter and open plan so that the kitchen was no longer a small isolated space with connotations of steam, grease and clattering pots. As the kitchen became part of a general family room its appearance also gradually improved.

Refrigerators replaced pantries; electric irons, washing machines and vacuum cleaners made housework less laborious and ready-made or convenience foods and breakfast cereals took the pressure off cooking, which it turn saw an increase in leisure time. This free time was used to listen to records from the burgeoning rock-and-roll industry or to go to a coffee bar with friends. It was the time of consumerism – objects were designed to be fashionable instead of just useful and there was a degree of built-in obsolescence so that gadgets could and would be replaced by the next new thing.

Television was making its way into homes and became not only a source of news and entertainment but also a marketing tool, which in turn made packaging and label design more important. Some brands, such as Coca-Cola, produced glasses and other wares that were collected and displayed in homes.

In 1957 the Soviet Union put a Sputnik into space, which fuelled an interest in science fiction, and this also had an influence on design. George Nelson's distinctive atomic ball clock and Bertoia's innovative wire Diamond chair for Knoll both date from this rich period.

Things American also had a big impact on Britain and Europe, not just the rock-and-roll and pop culture but also the big screen movies, which fuelled a desire for glamour. The average homeowner could not afford silk satin and velvet, but synthetic, manmade materials such as nylon and polyester could be used to create the look.

With this explosion of pattern, colour and advertising wares to choose from there is a danger of slipping into an odd design genre of the time, kitsch. The word 'kitsch' described the bold and sometimes garish patterns and design excesses of the fifties. It is a style or look that can be gaudy and overpowering if taken to extremes, but for some it is a tongue-in-cheek style of its own and if well put together it can be amusing.

When styling a retro kitchen try to choose, where possible, period-appropriate materials. Bakelite, melamine and plastic are all of this era. Aluminium was widely used for pots and pans as well as storage, but recently it has fallen out of favour as a material for cooking vessels because of its health implications.

Plastics were on the increase and this was the heyday of the Tupperware party, the direct-marketing strategy whereby housewives hosted their friends at home and sold the storage system to them directly. This form of selling made the company's name and also saw millions of its products make their way into homes around the globe. Tupperware was produced in 1946, when Earl Silas Tupper, an inveterate inventor who worked for some time at Du Pont, created the Wonderbowl, an airtight container with a snap-on lid and 'burping seal'.

From his factory and office in Massachusetts, Tupper went on to develop a whole range of airtight household plastic containers and it is said that he designed every piece of Tupperware his company produced. Although Tupper sold his business in 1959

Fifties style

FAR LEFT The original ribbed glass door panels and worn paintwork testify to this storage unit's date and authenticity, while the top is used to display a collection of humorous and vintage ceramics.

LEFT In the post-war spirit of 'Make do and mend' an old tool cabinet has been recycled as a store cupboard and a vintage caged industrial light hangs from the ceiling nearby.

THIS PAGE Randomly positioned shades of floor tiles pick up on the colours of the units and furniture and break up the plainness of the other white surfaces.

and retired to a small island in Central America, the company still bears his name and today Tupperware Brands has a sales force in the region of 3 million in almost 100 countries.

Along with Tupperware, another key product of this period is Fiesta ware. Although it is claimed to have been the most popular American dinnerware ever, it was designed by an Englishman, Frederick Hurten Rhead, and made from 1936 until 1972 by the Homer Laughlin Pottery Company of Newell, West Virginia. In 1985 the management of New York store Bloomingdale's approached Homer Laughlin about reproducing the range for them to sell and a year later a dinnerware line, in a new range of colours and with an improved glaze, was launched and proved a great success.

Fiesta ware was originally made in five colours: orangey red, blue, yellow, green and cream, known as old ivory. In 1937 the then ultra fashionable shade of turquoise joined the palette. The design of the ware had an Art Deco reference, with its border of concentric circles that was echoed in the original packaging, which depicted a Spanish dancer dressed in a traditional Flamenco skirt showing many layers.

Home diner

ABOVE Although the shelving and painted brick walls conjure up a utilitarian, feel the colourful vintage chairs attract the eye and give the room a more memorable appearance.

RIGHT The old neon advertising sign not only adds light and mood to the room but also stamps a period feel, which gives an identity to an otherwise neutral scheme.

Another much-loved and collected china range from this period is Ridgway's 1957 Homemaker, with a pattern designed by Enid Seeney on shapes by Tom Arnold. This tableware was made by Ridgway Potteries Ltd, and retailed, cheaply and exclusively, through Woolworths stores. The distinctive black-and-white colouring of Seeney's transfer-printed pattern shows contemporary furniture and domestic objects, such as two-seat sofas and wire-legged plant stands.

The Midwinter Pottery, founded in Burslem, Stoke-on-Trent in 1910, became one of England's largest potteries and by the late 1930s had 700 employees. In the 1950s, under the leadership of the director Roy Midwinter, the company became one of the leading innovators in British tableware, employing noted ceramicists and designers, including Jessie Tait, whose mosaic-style Homespun, red-and-white polka-dot Domino and exotic Bali and Capri are still much sought after and collected.

Textiles were another important area where contemporary design became popular. Gone were the floral prints and chintz of the 1930s and 40s, and in came the abstract and avant garde, much inspired by the artists of the time such as Kandinsky and

Streamlined storage

ABOVE LEFT Enamelware, open shelves and the Victoriana-style decorative tile border all add to the period feel of this kitchen corner.

ABOVE A new-but-old-style storage unit for dried goods and ingredients with contemporary enamelware pots and tins above.

RIGHT White goods, such as refrigerators, can be bought with modern mechanical fittings but vintage exterior styling.

Chrome details

FAR LEFT This vintage dresser's decorative top panel and rounded centre section, reminiscent of an early juke box, along with its mirrored mid-section shelves and reflective concave handles, all add to its glamorous appearance

LEFT This style of chair, with its chrome frame and painted or lacquered seat, is an example of mass-produced, modernist design found not only in homes but also in the coffee bars and cafés of the late 1950s and early 60s.

Alexander Calder. Designer Lucienne Day created her brightly coloured Calyx print for the Festival of Britain in 1951 and in the following year received the International Design Award of the American Institute of Decorators. Many of her designs were sold through the Tottenham Court Road, London store Heal's, as was the work of other designers of the day, such as Michael O'Connell, David Whitehead and Dorothy Carr.

Lucienne's husband Robin designed furniture that utilized the latest metal and woodworking techniques available in factories. The pieces he created were lightweight and streamlined, which suited the new, smaller style of 1950s home. Among his iconic and still admired pieces are the beech-framed and moulded plywood seat Hillestack chair produced by Hille and the mass-produced, injection-moulded Polyprop chair.

Even flooring took to colour and pattern, with the easy-to-wash, low-maintenance vinyl and lino floorings being widely popular. For the more modest home, foot-square black-and-white tiles or plain but strongly coloured options were available, while for the more adventurous there were designs that offered large purple polka dots and even pink poodles.

The Reclaimed Kitchen

ABOVE Industrial scaffolding is recycled as shelf supports and a frame for the sink and worktop.

RIGHT The black doors are made from old exterior cladding and the door and drawer handles are Champagne corks.

The kitchen is an expensive room to furnish — you need plenty of storage, good appliances, durable flooring, effective wall covering and directional lighting. And if you don't want to be constantly repairing and replacing, these things need to be of good quality, which usually means that they are not at the cheaper end of the scale when it comes to buying them new.

But you can find good-quality materials that have been used before: often older pieces of furniture are made from solid wood, rather than a veneer or MDF; recycled floor tiles and wooden boards or parquet will also be sturdy and reliable. They may also have the added patina of wear and age giving a mellow, more relaxed appearance to a room.

By saving some of your budget on reclaimed furniture and fittings you may find that you have more to spend on new appliances and electrical goods, which will come with a guarantee and warranty and be simpler and safer to use.

It seems that when people move into a new home one of the first rooms they rip out and redo is the kitchen. There are many skips and trucks outside homes filled to the brim with unwanted fitted units, many still in good condition and with plenty of wear left in them. For anyone who is good at DIY and has a bit of imagination these units offer a golden opportunity because, as long as their structure is sound and in good order, they can be reused.

Negotiate either with the builder or homeowner to buy or remove the units you require to fit out your space. The majority of kitchen units are made to a standard size and manufactured en masse in factories. They can be added to an existing run without too much trouble, so you can pick up a couple of units from one place and a few others from another. The units can also be raised or lowered by means of small adjustable feet or on blocks of wood concealed behind a plinth, so that they can be made level with any existing cooker or worktop.

The things that really stamp a style on a kitchen are the unit doors and work surfaces. If you have bought a new home with a perfectly usable kitchen but ugly doors and a scratched and stained worktop, then all you need to do is replace them. Many architects and interior designers buy basic white or wood kitchen units from a wholesale or high street supplier, but then add new, stylish handles or knobs and a thick worktop. The expensive worktop is a bit of a designer cliché, but it does give a feeling of weight and luxury, and again there are tricks that can save on costs.

A thick section of MDF can be wrapped in a panel of zinc or stainless steel that is cut and moulded to fit, making a shiny, substantial and attractive worktop. Marble looks good and adds a feeling of quality to a kitchen, but it is expensive so select a particular 'show' area in which it can be used and displayed. A dominant position such as the top of an island unit or breakfast bar is ideal, while the working sections around the sink and hob or oven can be made from a cheaper stone or other material.

Whitewashed wood

RIGHT Aged wood panels have been used to make units doors and drawer fronts as well as to camouflage the fascias of the modern appliances, such as the refrigerator and dishwasher.

FAR RIGHT In this corner, blocks of recycled wood have been invisibly fixed to the wall to provide robust shelves; the lack of struts and supports prevents the shelves from appearing overpowering.

Salvage style

LEFT AND ABOVE The metal frame of this conservatory-style kitchen could have given it a starkly utilitarian appearance, endorsed by the trough-style sink, enamelled lampshades and hanging rails for utensils and pots. But the softly pleated striped cotton curtains at the side windows and unit fronts make it less hard.

RIGHT In this converted church the kitchen is made up of a number of freestanding cabinets and shelving units, with a trolley for vegetables and condiments that can be rolled from one area of workspace to another.

Old wood is worth searching for – railway sleepers, oak beams and scaffolding boards make good, substantial work and table tops as well as useful shelving. The panels from empty tea chests and industrial crates can be recycled as door fronts, and even old cladding or shingles can be cleaned up and sanded to make façades and facings. Power hosing and a rub-down with an industrial sander will bring new life to old wood and also give it a deep clean, but do protect your eyes and cover your nose and mouth when using this type of equipment.

As well as the boards that are used in scaffolding, the steel poles or tubes that support them can also be reclaimed for kitchen structures and as supports for shelving. Because of their robust construction the poles can hold up stout shelves laden with heavy cast-iron pots and pans, as well as stacks of plates and other tableware. The

modular system of joints and hinges that scaffolding involves is very adaptable and so can be arranged to hold a large sink or a section of worktop with a hob. The poles look good either polished up and shiny or left with a matt and worn appearance, depending on the look you are going for, but either way they should be well cleaned before being fitted into a kitchen environment.

When it comes to flooring you can opt for new materials that suit this style, such as poured concrete, or look for something that has history. Whether you choose to source your flooring through a reclamation yard or buy from an advertisement or on-line site you will first need to have an accurate idea of the quantity of material you will require. Specific quantities of aged and worn old bricks and flagstones that have been salvaged from a single location will have a similar colour hue and pattern of wear. It will be difficult to add a few new bricks or stones to extend this quantity without them jarring visually, so it is important to try to buy an ample amount for your needs from a single source whenever possible.

Wooden flooring, whether reclaimed from a school gymnasium, a hotel foyer, an old shop that is closing down or refurbishing, a chapel or someone's home, will also have a similar tone or hue across all the boards. It is possible to sand and stain new wooden

Solid stone

LEFT Reclaimed wood may be sanded to remove the top layer of stain, varnish or grime, leaving the newly exposed layer with a bright, fresh appearance, as on these cupboard doors.

RIGHT A stone sink once used in an agricultural or industrial setting can provide similar capacity as a modern double sink, but be more in keeping with a rustic setting.

Mix & match

RIGHT The unfitted kitchen lends itself more easily to being constructed from recycled and reclaimed materials. Here a table is used as a draining board and the ceramic sink is supported on a polished stone slab, while the pipe work is left exposed.

FAR RIGHT The seats around the table have an industrial heritage, shown by the cast-iron base and hard polished wooden seats and backs.

floorboards to make them match more closely with the old, but the surface texture of the new wood may need to be distressed to give it a worn and aged appearance. This can be done with a small hammer, metal-capped shoe heels or a length of chain repeatedly pressed or thumped against the surface. Try a test area on an offcut so that you can gauge the amount of pressure and repetitions before setting to work on the main planks.

You can also reclaim materials and component parts for different uses. For example, an old stone or zinc water trough from a farm could be used as a sink; a millstone as an unusual table top; old shop fittings and display cases as dressers; a length

of copper piping as a pole or rod from which to hang pots and pans with butcher's hooks; enamelled advertising hoardings as splashbacks. On a smaller scale, Champagne corks can even make surprisingly good door handles.

With used machines and equipment for the reclaimed kitchen, it is best to go to a reliable and trade-approved source. A number of manufacturers offer limited guarantees on items that are their own products, if they have refurbished or reconditioned them themselves. But if you are in any doubt, walk away. It is better to spend a little more on a new item than to risk countless call outs and repairs on something that looks stylish but doesn't function.

Some domestic machine such as AGA ranges and Rayburns are built to last for generations, but may fall out of fashion with a homeowner who finds them impractical for the more immediate demands of everyday, modern cooking, or expensive to run as a heating unit. So these can often be bought second-hand if that's what you want to as a centrepiece for your reclaimed kitchen, although they are heavy and will need to be dismantled for transporting, so factor delivery costs into your budget.

Restaurants come and go and often their fixtures and fittings are ripped out and sold – these are usually robust, of good quality and hard-wearing because they were designed for heavy daily use. As long as you have space to accommodate and do justice to these larger items they can be quite easily adapted to work in a domestic environment.

Glorious wood

RIGHT The floor, fitted units, freestanding chest of drawers and dining furniture form a ground base of a similar hue, while the white walls are partially concealed behind a classic gold-framed mirror and a mirror panel with section of glass shelving supported on industrial-style black brackets.

The White Kitchen

The white kitchen can be simple or sophisticated, minimalist or vintage style, because white is an anonymous and multifunctional shade. White is not actually a colour — colours are made because rays of coloured light are absorbed into an object. With white all the coloured rays are reflected.

White is often used to complement the stainless-steel surfaces in a professional kitchen; it reflects light and gives a plain background against which many colourful and flavoursome dishes can be created. White is also associated with purity and cleanliness, so has a direct link to hygiene, important in the storing and preparation of food.

Some modern paints incorporate reflective elements that make a white surface appear more brilliant, although this can create glare and be hard on the eyes. There are also many commercially produced 'shades of white', some tinted with blue making them cool and fresh, or yellow for a warmer, creamier effect.

ABOVE In this windowless cavern-like room the white walls and floor help to reflect the light coming from the doorway.

RIGHT Walls, floor, ceiling and furniture all painted in a mellow off-white give a small room a fresh, bright appearance.

THIS PAGE In this predominantly modern and bright-white kitchen a row of well-polished classic copper pans makes an eye-catching and colourful feature.

Pale panelling

LEFT Painted tongue-and-groove cladding provides heat and noise insulation as well as a sturdy wall finish. The paint seals and protects the wood, making it easy to wipe clean.

RIGHT This scullery-style kitchen has only two narrow, high windows from which to access daylight, so a white scheme helps to brighten its appearance.

The versatility and timelessness of white mean it can be used on many different surfaces and finishes, from cabinet doors and worktops, to floors and walls and even fabrics. The advantage to this neutral base is that it can easily be touched up or repainted, or in the case of fabric washed and even bleached to bring back its freshness.

For a country style or an authentic traditional kitchen the walls could be painted with a white distemper, an ancient type of paint made of water, chalk and pigment bound together with an adhesive made from either animal glue or milk solids. This type of paint is inexpensive but not long-lasting and may become powdery and brush off the wall onto clothes. Another traditional white paint is whitewash, or lime paint made from chalk and slaked lime. It was traditionally used in food preparation areas, particularly rural dairies, because of its mildly antibacterial properties. And whitewash was also used historically, both externally and internally, in workers' cottages.

Though both distemper and whitewash were widely used until the end of the nineteenth century, the arrival of oil- and latex-based house paints saw them fall out of favour. But an increased interest in using authentic period finishes and environmental concerns about chemical-based decorating products has seen a recent revival in their use.

Modern more stable paints include emulsion, vinyl and gloss. Vinyl finishes are easy to wipe clean and therefore good for walls near the hob and sink where splashes may occur, and gloss dries to a tough hard shine, which makes it good for painting floorboards or other areas of high use.

Tongue-and-groove panelling on walls provides good sound and heat insulation and is a useful way of covering up or protecting an area where the wall surface is less than perfect. If the wood being used for this type of finish is new it should be sealed with an undercoat before the top layer is applied;

China & glass

LEFT With its association with cleanliness and purity white is an ideal shade for a kitchen, but avoid a sterile appearance by adding other, warmer, materials such as wood.

BELOW Glistening glassware and shining silver will stand out wonderfully against a plain white background, especially when displayed on open shelves.

RIGHT The pale grey of the wall highlights the white wares arranged on the plain shelves in front.

this will prevent any resin or knots from marking the finish. Raw or new plaster walls should also be sealed with a primer or base coat before painting. But be careful when touching up white paintwork because you may find that the existing paint has yellowed or aged, so that the new white paint will look overly bright when it is applied on an adjacent area. Always try a test patch in a discreet, out-of-the-way corner to make sure the whites are compatible before embarking on a repair mission.

White is also used when referring to machines and appliances found in the kitchen. White goods such as refrigerators, washing machines, dishwashers and driers were originally finished only in white enamel and despite the fact that they are now available in a variety of colours they are still referred to as white goods. In some countries domestic textiles, such as tablecloths and towels, which were also traditionally white, are also referred to as white goods.

White enamel was a popular finish for pots, pans, utensils and bakeware. For over 200 years the Austrian, family-owned business Riess has been making this type of kitchen product. The process is still artisan-based, with each pot being shaped from a single piece of steel, then hand sprayed with four coats of glass enamel before being baked in vast kilns. The result is a non-porous container with good heat conductivity, which makes it suitable for use with induction, gas, wood or electric cookers or stovetops. But when cooking with enamelware it is recommended that you only use silicone or wooden cooking implements to prevent the surface from being scratched.

Another company that has been making enamelware for generations is Falcon Enamelware. Since the 1920s its iconic ware in white with a distinctive blue rim has been made by fusing a porcelain finish onto heavy-gauge steel, making a smooth durable surface that is dishwasher- and oven-safe.

As well as enamelware, wood, steel, china and glass are also good materials with which to dress the white kitchen. Large amounts of copper could be overpowering because its rich colouring and the shine will be in direct contrast to the simplicity of the surroundings. Well-polished brass, used for taps and hinges, handles and knobs, can be attractive because the colouring is more subtle and yellow than copper, but if you choose to have these metal fixtures they must be kept shiny and well polished to look their best.

White is also the favoured shade for mass-produced china and tableware, and because of the wide availability of this plain commodity it tends to be inexpensive and easy to replace. And the neutral colour is an effective linking factor between all sorts of items. You don't have to match the shape and make of white tableware – you could mix vintage side plates that have a scalloped edge with dinner plates or bowls with a smooth flat

Elegant dining

FAR LEFT In this kitchen a variety of styles and periods, from the rustic shelves and archways to the modern rounded wall shelves and contemporary furniture, are brought together by the common theme of white.

LEFT A monochrome scheme bringing together the contrasting shades of black and white can look crisp and smart, and will work for a number of styles including Art Deco and modernist.

RIGHT Different areas of use in this large open-plan space are made compatible by being themed around shades of the same colour.

rim, and modern with antique. White always makes a good background to any dish or meal because there are no colours or patterns to distract from the food – it is like a blank canvas onto which the colours and textures can be applied or arranged to best effect.

The simplicity of a white kitchen also means that the eye is drawn to the detail. The lack of distraction by colour and pattern means that the line and style of the room becomes prominent, so features such as panelling, trim, cupboard and drawer handles, as well as the fittings and furnishings, are all important. Edges of worktops should be well finished and the materials themselves, such as white marble or zinc, of good quality. Fixtures, such as a white ceramic Belfast sink or a row of lime-washed shelves, should be carefully selected and positioned.

Fabrics also play an important part in the look of the *Kitchenalia* white kitchen. You can break up the severity of a white room with interesting textures and vintage cloths. For example, a gingham curtain or table cloth that might also coordinate with a small collection of white and red or white and blue china. The density of the fabric may also dictate how and where it is used – for example, fine white voile or cheesecloth is light and airy, making it ideal for curtains, while calico or cotton may be denser and therefore useful as cushion or seat covers, or curtains that disguise open shelves.

Another area of textiles that is worth investigating for this type of kitchen is the antique or vintage cloths from European countries. For example, the French have a rich heritage of linen tea towels, known as *torchon*. These classic, stout linen drying cloths have a classic red stripe and make an interesting and practical addition when hung from a peg rail or butcher's hook. They can be used as a linen tea towel or, as

Kitchen corners

ABOVE RIGHT Small spaces will appear roomier if well lit and decorated in a single plain colour.

RIGHT Even a utilitarian wood store built into a corner can be made to look bright and fresh when painted white.

THIS PAGE White needs to be well maintained to stay looking this good, but it is easy to touch up paint and to wash down vinyl or gloss finishes in areas of frequent use and wear.

the French do, as a generous individual napkin. Another cloth is the *métis*, a kitchen towel that was part of a traditional French trousseau, often embroidered with the bride's initials and with woven red or blue stripes or bands down each side.

Although white provides a light-reflective surface it will need to be supplemented by electric task and decorative lighting. But if your kitchen is in a particularly sunny position you may also need blinds or curtains to help reduce glare and to keep the room cool when the sun shines in directly and for a prolonged period. In keeping with enamel bakeware, you can also find industrial-style white enamel light shades; these are hard-wearing and easy to clean, but be careful when touching them after the light has been on for some time because the shades themselves will become, and stay, hot.

With a white kitchen it is vital that it stays white – nothing shows up grime and damage more than a plain white background. So the white kitchen is a demanding space, but a rewarding one because when it looks good, it looks magnificent.

White canvas

LEFT A ceramic Belfast sink blends in with the single colour theme of this room, whereas a modern stainless-steel version may have jarred.

ABOVE RIGHT Smart white fabric curtains conceal the contents of the shelves behind them. They should be regularly taken down and washed to maintain their pristine and crisp appearance.

RIGHT Shades of white and off-white can be used together to give a little variation and interest in a larger room.

The Painted Kitchen

The *Kitchenalia* painted kitchen creates a statement using colour, colour that makes a strong impact rather than a background wash or muted tone. As well as adding to the personality and visual appeal of your kitchen, paint is a useful way of sealing and finishing surfaces, and if you use a water-resistant paint such as a vinyl or gloss finish, it will be washable as well as hard-wearing.

With reclaimed or old wooden furniture and units part of the revamping process may involve sanding or stripping off the original finish and making repairs. Once that is done you can set about applying a bright fresh coat of paint or stain. The paint you choose should be stable, so probably best to avoid the chalk-based varieties. Although they have a lovely soft, velvety appearance, they may absorb grease splashes and marks and brush off, leaving dusty marks on your clothes and furniture.

ABOVE LEFT Colour may be used to distinguish or identify different cupboards or units and their contents.

LEFT Different styles of old wooden chairs are united by a coat of the same pastel shade of green paint.

RIGHT The warm tones of the aubergine and pink painted on the chairs help to warm up the cool grey of the rest of the room.

Shades of blue

ABOVE The vibrant red of the walls inside this pantry contrast strongly with the cool turquoise blue of the door frame and panels, all of which draws the eye to the china on display.

ABOVE RIGHT This soft blue contains a large percentage of white in its composition so that it is compatible, rather than a contrast, with the white walls and floor.

Paint has magical properties when it comes to decorating. It can be used to transform a dull piece of furniture into something exciting, to make an odd piece blend in with others or to alter the perception of its size and stature. You may come across a useful but rather mundane cupboard made of a standard yellow pine, chipboard or MDF, or a mix of modern kitchen units with a featureless façade. By painting these pieces of furniture a bright or interesting colour and adding decorative beading and unusual handles, they could be transformed.

In a kitchen that is short on storage, you could use an expanse of empty wall for a dresser or set of shelves, employing colour to make odd or disparate pieces of furniture blend together. For example, if you have a low-level cupboard pushed against a wall and a wall-mounted glass-fronted unit above it, by painting both pieces the same colour you will visually link the two, so they will appear more like a dresser.

THIS PAGE This vibrant blue helps to reduce the height and volume of the room, giving it a warmer, more intimate appearance. The colour is echoed in the storage jars and the tile border.

THIS PAGE Although black is a shade that would be difficult to use on its own in a kitchen, when teamed with white it creates a smart and distinctive appearance. This contrasting backdrop works well with stainless-steel and chrome accessories and machines.

Moody monochrome

ABOVE Because grey is made by mixing black and white it is always compatible with white. But avoid sludgy hues because they may appear grubby instead of smoky.

ABOVE RIGHT The sink's splashback is faced with varying shades of grey slate, which bring together the white of the walls and sink and the black of the smart painted units.

You could also paint the section of wall between the units in the same shade and that would make it appear even more unified. If you have gone for an unfitted look and have lots of different styles of cabinets and units, painting them all the same colour will bring cohesion to a look that could otherwise look rather jumbled. A set of chairs made up of two or three different styles can be painted in shades that either pair up the matching ones, or make a feature of the fact that they are odd or different styles.

Use colour creatively to play with space. A large cupboard or unit can appear smaller and less intrusive if painted in a pale or light colour, or a shade that blends with the surrounding wall. A small but attractive cupboard can be made more noticeable if painted in a bright or contrasting colour to its background. You can also use colour to create a feeling of depth. If you have a dresser with shallow shelves, paint the backboard in a dark colour and it will seem further away, and conversely with deep shelves paint the back white or a light colour to make it seem closer.

As well as paint you can also colour wooden furniture and floors with stains. Stains come in standard wood shades that mimic cherry, walnut and oak, as well as paint-pot colours such as red and blue. You can use stencils and stamps to make repeat patterns

Multicoloured storage

LEFT Use dark and rich colours only in a bright and well-lit kitchen, otherwise they can make the room feel small, stuffy and claustrophobic.

RIGHT White-based shades of pale green are fresh and zesty and useful to lift the appearance of a small or dark room.

or borders and monograms as a decorate motif. Many stains also contain wood preservative so will help to maintain the structure of the wood, but if there are signs of woodworm or rot it is advisable to treat these problems separately before carrying out any decoration. If in doubt call on professional help.

Paint doesn't have to be applied in smooth and even coats. You can water it down to get a wash of colour that adds a tonal shade but still allows the attractive wood grain to show through. Or apply a base coat of one colour with a top coat of another and sand off parts of the upper colour to reveal patches of the colour below, creating a weathered or aged look. Paint can also be applied with a dry brush dipped lightly into the paint then quickly swept or stroked across the surface for a streaky, almost grained effect, or apply the paint with a dryish sponge for a softer, mottled finish.

Preparation before painting is important, especially if restoring an old piece of furniture. You will need to strip or sand off the existing varnish or paint to create a smooth and absorbent surface for the new finish. Old peeling paint may look attractive, but in a kitchen it can be unhygienic and flakes might to fall into food, so sand down the rough edges and seal the surface with a clear varnish or seal that will set and stabilize the paintwork.

Another effective area to use colour is as a splashback around a sink or work area. Colour can be introduced by painting the wall and then protecting it with a panel of clear glass, or in some cases you can buy glass that already has a painted back. If that doesn't appeal you can achieve a similar effect with a couple of rows of boldly coloured ceramic tiles.

ABOVE The powder blue of the refrigerator has been matched in the paintwork of a recycled storage cabinet.

RIGHT Two different-sized wall units are painted the same shade to give them a more uniform appearance.

The Country Kitchen

Even in the most modern and metropolitan city you will find kitchens styled to give the appearance of being in the depths of the country, somewhere far removed from the sirens of police cars and ambulances, and the bustle of the sidewalk.

This type of kitchen encapsulates a relaxed and easy-going lifestyle and features subtle washes of nature-inspired colours. Basketwork, wood and copper are all ingredients that will help to create the look, and for the *Kitchenalia* country kitchen vintage and traditional elements are important.

The country kitchen is designed to be used. It is a place to cook, preserve and bottle, where bowls are licked and the smell of fresh bread tempts people in. It is at heart a family space, a social hub where people meet and chat, often around the stove or range whose constant heat is used to warm and dry.

ABOVE LEFT Unadorned white walls with a wood floor and furnishings contribute a simple, rustic appearance to this unfitted kitchen.

LEFT By keeping the original deep hearth and chimney breast the historic elements of this room have been preserved and utilized.

RIGHT Rough plaster walls, old wooden beams and a stone floor are all classic elements of the traditional country-style kitchen.

French style

RIGHT Blue-and-white checked seat covers on well-turned chairs, decorative shelf brackets and a Lacanche-style cooker create a more sophisticated, French-style country look.

FAR RIGHT Although there are contemporary elements in this room, such as the breakfast bar and wall-hung radiator, they are offset by raffia seat chairs with Shaker-style ladder backs and a stone floor.

LIBRAIRIE-

BREAD

Country style does not have one single set of design rules; it is a look that can be interpreted in many ways, each subtly different and adaptable to your home and requirements. If you live in a modern city apartment you are unlikely to have beams, a hearth or fireplace or even space to suspend a hanging clothes drier from the ceiling, so in that situation you could look to a pared-down and simpler country style for inspiration, for example the Shaker community.

The Shakers were a religious group founded in the 1770s by Mother Ann Lee who, with her followers, left Manchester in England to settle in America. They lived in communities and made their own wooden furniture, often in maple and cherry, which was simple and functional, but of high quality because of their belief that all their work was a testament to God.

They also believed that every object should be functional and that extraneous decoration was unnecessary, although they did occasionally use a simple hand and heart motif representing their motto 'hands to work and heart to God'. They employed a limited palette of colours – ox-blood red, a soft grey blue, yellow and sage green – often made from plant and other natural dyestuffs, but which are very attactive in themselves.

The furniture was arranged in open uncluttered rooms with whitewashed walls and wooden floors. Cleanliness was very important to the Shakers, so things were stored away neatly and out of sight in chests, boxes and baskets, and furniture was light and easy to move. Their trademark ladder-back chairs were often hung up on peg rails when they weren't in use so that the floors could be thoroughly swept.

Rustic charm

LEFT Wood and baskets create a relaxed and lived-in feeling. Here roughly hewn, handmade boards for serving cheeses and dried meats are hung beneath a shelf that supports storage bottles and creamware bowls.

RIGHT Handmade rustic plates and bowls with a traditional yellow glaze are practical and attractive, and also contribute to the decor of the room when arranged on a simple dresser.

This simple, more streamlined version of the country look, or an interpretation of it that follows the Shaker injunctions rather more fluidly than the original inflexible strictures, works well in small rooms and apartments. Some contemporary kitchen companies produce units and fixtures in this style, so the basics can be bought ready-made. Genuine Shaker furniture is now much sought after and collected, so expensive, but the look can be achieved with modern reproductions.

The Shaker-inspired kitchen is closely linked in looks to classic Gustavian and Scandinavian styles, but instead of the strong nature-based colours, the coolness of the northern light is reflected in lighter shades such as grey and lavender blue, and fabrics may be more decorative, typically featuring small floral prints or checks.

The Gustavian kitchen has a more country or manor house feel, with formal furniture and decorative ware, whereas the rural idyll, such as seen in the work of the Swedish artist Carl Larsson, is more Arts and Crafts inspired, with wood panelling, shelves supported by decorated brackets and piled with plates and china. Window boxes of herbs or pots of bright red geraniums, which feature in many of Larsson's paintings, are also a clever way of bringing the 'country' indoors.

Clean lines

RIGHT This Scottish-themed country kitchen uses tartan-decorated china and a plaid cloth to evoke a sense of place. Whitewashed walls, a scrubbed pine table and the dresser are anonymous in tone so the accessories create the style.

FAR RIGHT Simplicity and functionality are the focus of this scheme – the gleaming stainless-steel work surfaces add a contemporary edge, but the roller towel on the back of the door adds a timeless feel.

For larger rooms and more full-scale country kitchen, it is worth investigating regional or rural styles from other countries. For example, a Scottish take on country style could feature local elements such as tartan and horn, granite and heathery tones, while a French country style might focus on red-and-white check or gingham, old Pastis signs or posters as well as armoires and cabinets with worn and weathered paint.

If the gingham or check look appeals it doesn't need to be only used in fabrics – you could also make a panel of red-and-white or blue-and-white square ceramic tiles as a splashback behind the sink or around the oven or stove, making this area the focal point. Or decorate your floor in a chequerboard pattern, using either tiles or a painted design on wooden floorboards.

For flooring and worktops look at vernacular materials – for example, in a French-inspired county kitchen French limestone or, if heading further around the Mediterranean for inspiration, handmade Italian terracotta floor tiles and small square ceramic wall tiles in an array of rich jewel colours.

When it comes to decorating the walls consider what you already have. If the plasterwork or render is firm and in good order then it may be a matter of freshening it up with paint, wallpaper or tiles. If the surface is not in good condition, having been drilled or filled with picture hooks and bracket screws, or if you want a really rustic feel, then you could remove the plaster and expose the brickwork. But do check first that you have bricks and not ugly grey breeze blocks behind the plaster.

Hearth & home

THIS PAGE Architectural features, such as this deeply recessed hearth and substantial mantel, can be the focus of a room, and may also dictate or contribute to the overall choice of decorative style.

RIGHT This old cast-iron range is still in use and evokes a deep sense of history.

Another option is to cover up the wall with tongue-and-groove or flat wooden panelling, whichever is more appropriate to your chosen style and the age of the building in which you live. You could also strip and replaster the walls, and then you have the option of leaving the soft beige pink plaster as it is or adding a coat of seal or undercoat before painting a plain colour or adding a wash of paint-effect finish.

Kitchenalia kitchen style is about mixing and matching, it is not a uniform look that can be bought off a shelf, but one that takes time to create and to select the right elements. In fact, with this loose approach you could opt for a general, Mediterranean country style rather than focusing on one specific country. Think of sunshine, blue skies and olive trees, baskets of ripe tomatoes and green glass bottles filled with local wine and beer. Then pick out the best elements from various countries and bring them together with a uniform backdrop of white or off-white walls, simple units and a sturdy floor covering.

The danger with *Kitchenalia* country style is overdoing it. Try and be disciplined and hang a few useful baskets on the wall rather than a stack that will gather dust and cobwebs. A good guideline is 'don't keep it if you don't use it', although there may be exceptions for a much-treasured collection of china

or olive-wood chopping boards, which can be made part of the decoration of the room. And remember that the kitchen is a place where food is stored and prepared so do not clutter up worktops and tables so much that these primary functions are difficult to perform. And with arrangements of baskets, wood and materials such as curtains and cloth it is important to ensure that the room and the area above the hob or stove is well ventilated so that moisture doesn't accumulate and dampen or cause rot in these objects.

An authentic country-house kitchen would have had space to accommodate a large range or fireplace, a long scrubbed-pine table and flagstone floors. The hanging clothes drier above the stove and a mantelpiece are all useful, but if your kitchen is small just scale things down and create a focus with a large chimney canopy or extractor cover and a chunky wooden shelf.

If you have inherited a perfectly serviceable fitted kitchen that you don't want the expense or inconvenience of replacing, create a country style with the detail and fabrics, such as old French linen tea towels and canister storage labelled *Sucre* and *Farine*, instead of sugar and flour. Look for these in markets and *brocantes* while on holiday in France or through internet sites. If you have space also add a few pieces of unfitted furniture such as a butcher's block, trolley or series of open shelves, to break up the uniformity of the built-in units.

Bringing together your own mix of furniture will also help; old wooden chairs with raffia seats, a round gate-legged table with a simple white tablecloth and a collection of cream china in a dresser can soften and counteract even the most contemporary-style units. The important thing is to keep it simple and to create an atmosphere that is laid-back and informal.

Warm wood

ABOVE Around the walls of this room, the tops of the stone-built benches act as work surfaces, while wine and wood are stored in the spaces below.

RIGHT The cream-painted wooden panelling and simple, uncluttered lines of this room give it an historic and Shaker-style appearance.

The Collector's Kitchen

This type of kitchen can be combined with other looks, including some found in previous chapters of *Kitchenalia*. For example, if you have a collection of earthenware pots and old baskets you may choose a country kitchen in which to exhibit them, or a collection of brightly coloured melamine tableware and a trio of George Nelson clocks might lead you into the realms of a retro-inspired scheme.

For more general collections, of jugs, copper pans or blue-and-white china say, not of a certain period or particular style, a supportive but subtle decorative scheme is usually the answer. The furniture in which the collection is arranged, or the wall or shelf where it is displayed, will be of primary importance. With a large collection, especially of patterned china, it is best to keep the decorative style simple so that it doesn't compete with the arrangement or dilute its impact.

ABOVE LEFT A collection of colourful toy cookers and stoves add a touch of humour to a white-painted mantel.

RIGHT A diverse range of china in different styles and from various periods is arranged on an open dresser and is the focal point of the room.

There are three types of collector's kitchens. The first is where the objects are on display and regularly used, the second is where the collection is primarily for decorative display purposes, and the third is a mix of both use and display.

The kitchen where the collection is in daily use will have display areas that are easily accessible, whereas the solely display collection may feature rows of jugs high up on the top of a dresser or plates grouped on a wall and hung from plate-hanging racks or fixed clips. The third type of collector's kitchen, which is probably the most common, will have a combination of both. The 'used' collection is usually made up of things that look attractive but are not precious or irreplaceable, whereas the purely display collection may include rare and special or limited edition pieces, as well as some things that are beautiful but fragile or damaged, so no longer capable of withstanding the rigours of use.

Decorative effect

ABOVE Old enamelware makes an interesting display when ranged along a dividing wall. These containers are chipped and would therefore be unhygienic to use, but still make an attractive group.

RIGHT A collection of religious-themed paintings provides an interesting backdrop. Old oil paintings, found at car boot sales and flea markets, are fairly resilient to the steam and heat of the kitchen.

Grouping objects

ABOVE Ridgway's Homemaker china is combined with some plain black and similar-styled black-and-white designs to make a mix-and-match collection.

ABOVE RIGHT A collection of decorative plates is arranged and hung on the wall as a feature above a doorway.

RIGHT Vintage signs and an unusual stepped shelf spice rack make an interesting and useful display near this stove.

To display your collection or collections in an interesting and attractive way it is worth taking time to test and trial various arrangements. First of all take a long hard look at your kitchen and how you can use what is available, identifying usable wall area with sufficient height and space so that items arranged there won't be in the way or likely to be damaged by heat from a stove or steam. If you have uneven or springy flooring then you will need to level out a freestanding dresser or secure it to the wall so that it doesn't rock or shake when people walk by, setting all your painstakingly amassed china rattling or threatening to slip.

For the maximum visual impact try to focus the main part of your display at eye level, rather than high up or low down where it might be overlooked. Then analyse your collection and decide whether you should have one large focal point, say a dresser, or

FAR LEFT Vintage china, some usable, other pieces for display only, are arranged on a classic, painted wooden dresser.

LEFT Taxidermy makes an unusual wall dressing. Here the pieces are contained within glass-fronted, sealed boxes to protect them from steam and grease.

a couple of smaller groups – for example, a cluster of decorative side plates linked by a colour theme displayed on the wall, with a row of vintage glasses on a shelf above or nearby. A large quantity of a certain object, such as jugs and pitchers, or a particular type of china, can be very impressive, but be careful to keep the overall size of the arrangement in proportion so that it doesn't overwhelm a small kitchen or get lost in a large one.

Once you have identified the area in which your collection will be located then look at the different display options. If you are using deep shelves or a dresser then you could experiment with layering, for a dense display. Place plates upright against the back of the shelf, then a row of medium-sized cream jugs in front and finally, between the jugs and to the edge of the shelf, add smaller items such as egg cups or mustard, salt and pepper pots. You can also group things according to shape or use, so

a row of identical herb or spice containers, for example, or a cluster of copper jelly moulds will create their own visual entity. Colour or pattern can also be used as a unifying theme for a collection; green glass bottles in various hues and sizes will look stronger when grouped together, as will a cluster of creamware plates and platters of various sizes and shapes, but sharing the same off-white glaze.

For collections displayed on single narrow shelves or mantelpieces think of the overall shape of the items on show. Try putting the tallest piece, such as a large coffee pot, in the middle then graduate the other objects outwards on either side, so that they decrease in stature until the smallest items are at either end of the shelf. This will create a key central point and then a smooth line for the eye to follow, so the individual pieces themselves can be appreciated.

Shape is also important in bringing together a collection of random items. You can either arrange them within the confines or frame of an architectural feature in the room, such as a chimney breast or an alcove, or create a theoretical shape such as a circle or square. By arranging the objects within the feature or perceived delineation of the shape you will create a group that is visually more pleasing to the eye than random gathering, which can look like clutter.

Vary the density of a display by interrupting a row of richly coloured and patterned objects with a group of glasses or plain white or cream china; think of it as a pause in a conversation. If you have a particularly special piece of china such as a cup and saucer or a silver jug you can 'frame' it by placing it in front of an upright white plate that has a gilded or silvered edge, or is in a plain but contrasting colour.

Any collection should be securely arranged so that it is safe – both from breakages and from causing damage or injury if pieces should be accidentally dislodged. Brass or steel hooks are a useful way of doubling up shelf space and ideal for suspending items with handles such as cups, mugs and small jugs. You can also screw them to the front edge of a dresser shelf or under a single wall-mounted shelf for longer and larger items, such as baskets, utensils or dried flowers and herbs. To display flat items such as plates you can buy wire plate hangers that clip onto the foot at the back of the plate, or stick on hooks that are ideal for smaller, lightweight china. Shelves of

Beautiful blue & white

LEFT & ABOVE Plates displayed in the upright position should be set into a niche or recess cut into the upper side of the shelf, or be secured by a small ball of putty-like material at their base to prevent them slipping.

RIGHT Hand-painted lines on the shelf edge and a key motif on the adjacent wall pick up on the colour and loose style of the decoration on this collection of wares.

Prized china

ABOVE Plain plates and servers of different shapes and sizes but similar colours are arranged as an elegant focal point on a plain wall.

ABOVE RIGHT The dark wood back wall of this richly coloured cabinet enhances the jewel-like colours and dense patterns of the china displayed within.

RIGHT Creamware was made by factories such as Belleek and Wedgwood. Josiah Wedgwood, who supplied Queen Charlotte and Catherine the Great, also used the trade name Queen's ware.

purpose-built display units and dressers often have a narrow indent into which the rim of an upright plate can be slotted to prevent it sliding and give stability. You can also buy small, individual ornate corbels that will support a single object. These can be used to show off one special item, or arranged in a group to form a collective display.

The one golden rule for the collector's kitchen is that once or twice a year any items that haven't been in regular use must be taken down and cleaned, and the shelves wiped down to prevent accumulations of dust and grease. In the case of metals such as copper or silver-cleaning will need to be even more frequent to maintain the surface shine. Dull and tarnished pieces will spoil the look of your carefully constructed array. A useful tip is that before dismantling your display take a couple of photographs so that when you come to put everything back you have a record of where it came from.

On the wall

LEFT A collection of decorative copper cake and jelly moulds make an interesting and unusual wall-hung group.

THIS PAGE A wooden paddle used to insert bread or pizza into a wood-burning oven is surrounded by a pewter dish dome and other kitchenalia.

MESS

N° 19

The Utilitarian Kitchen

The utilitarian kitchen has an uncluttered, practical appearance focusing on a no-nonsense design aesthetic. It is about form and function, and borrows heavily from the utilitarian considerations found in industrial design. It also has roots in the era after World War II when materials were in short supply, so furniture became pared-down and simple, much inspired by the streamlined shapes of Scandinavian design.

The spartan style of the 1950s was also influenced by the trend for moderne, or what is now more commonly called mid-century modern design, a style that used dramatic planes and geometric shapes rather than ornate detail. Light woods such as pine, ash and birch were popular, as were 'manufacturing' materials such as zinc and stainless steel. Also borrowing from industry, mobility is often a feature, with tables and benches fitted with lockable wheels.

ABOVE LEFT This pared-down, simple kitchen is functional and unfussy, but still has elements of warmth and comfort.

LEFT A basic steel-framed breakfast bar, with similar lines to an industrial workbench, fits neatly into a corner.

RIGHT The utilitarian kitchen focuses on function ,which makes it a good style guide for small spaces.

Workroom

LEFT Industrial enamel light shades, a metal frame workbench used as an island unit and a large cooker hood all contribute to the work-focused appearance of this galley-style kitchen.

RIGHT The blackboard-painted wall gives this room something of a school-laboratory appearance, which is also endorsed by the solid recycled wooden bench on wheels and ceiling-hung, pendant metal lampshades.

The utilitarian kitchen is inspired by the 1950s, a time when architecture was embracing new, modern styles of domestic building with large windows, allowing plenty of access to natural light, and a reduction in the number of small, individual rooms. This in turn led to the creation of open floor plans so that the kitchen became larger and connected with other activities, such as eating or relaxing.

More likely to be pieced together from individual machines and pieces of furniture, the utilitarian kitchen is not fitted out with wall-to-wall units. The industrial look will be built up from a combination of workbenches, island stations and easy-to-clean surfaces. Think of strong, well-designed pieces, fit for purpose and void of ornamentation.

Then add a little of the warmth of wood and organic shapes from the Scandinavian designers and manufacturers who were influential in the 1950s, many of whose designs are still in production to this day. Scandinavian design is characterized by simplicity and flowing natural forms that can be seen in the work of the Finns Alvar and Aino Aalto and the glassware company Iittala. Danish designers including Georg Jensen, Hans Wegner, Verner Panton and Poul Henningsen also produced furniture and lighting that are still found in many contemporary homes.

At its factory in Gothenburg the Swedish company Electrolux produced its first home washing machine in 1951, and eight years later it was joined by a counter-top

Cooked Prawn Risoni
bag of peas
small can sweet corn (drained)
2 sticks celery diced
small onion (diced & sauté
in olive oil till
caramelised)
cooked prawns
hand full chopped parsley

mix all ingredients & season
well with salt & pepper

LEFT Oblong white ceramic tiles and a couple of simple hanging rails for pots and pans are both elements that could be found in a professional restaurant or hotel kitchen.

RIGHT This type of stamped metal ceiling covering was found in the industrial warehouses of New York and other Victorian industrial hubs. The look can be replicated by painting Anaglypta wallpaper with silver paint.

dishwasher nicknamed the 'round jar'. These advancements and wider availability of household appliances also brought a more mechanized look to the kitchen. The trend carries on in the modern utilitarian kitchen, where many of the machines and appliances are industrial, sourced from hotel and restaurant suppliers, or styled by domestic manufacturers to have the robust, no-frills look of commercial machines.

As well as steel cookers, sinks and work surfaces some smaller appliances and fixtures have also crossed the divide. For example, the nozzle-spout style of tap on a flexible hose, once used for washing catering pans, is now found above family kitchen sinks being used to clean off the pots and pans from Sunday lunch or the barbecue grill. Steam ovens and pantry-sized fridges and freezers as well as rubber and stamped metal flooring all have their roots in industrial settings but have made their way into the domestic arena.

Although the Scandinavians are an important influence, there were other manufacturers who produced wares that are suited to the utilitarian kitchen. In 1930 an American, Edwin Knowles, started the Knowles China Company in Chester, West Virginia. The plant manufactured semi-porcelain items of toilet ware, kitchenware and dinnerware, and in 1938 produced a modern, streamlined range of products known as Utility Ware, which came in a choice of solid colours, or white with a coloured trim.

Meanwhile, in Sausalito, California, industrial designer and potter Edith Heath was establishing her business Heath Ceramics. The company became well known for its simple and durable mid-century modern wares and architectural tiles, which were used in homes as well as commercial restaurants. Eighty years later the company still follows the simplicity of the shapes and structure she pioneered, and original pieces of Heath Ceramics can be found in use in many kitchens across America.

Metallic edge

THIS PAGE Although there is a country-style wall rack and cupboard in this room the large steel cooker and fridge-freezer give it a harder edge, heightened by the expanse of blackboard-painted wall.

RIGHT Black rubber waste bins and the steel-fronted sink area contribute to the crisp industrial appearance. The space between the two sides of the room also gives unhindered access to the main machines.

Fellow Californians Charles and Ray Eames were designing streamlined furniture that could be mass-produced in factories, at the same time as Heath was developing her minimal, modern pottery shapes. The husband and wife team experimented with new techniques and materials that were being developed at the time and used them in their indoor-outdoor collection of aluminium furniture and fibreglass Shell chairs.

Lighting in this style of kitchen draws directly from the factories and machine rooms of the 1940s and 50s, and although originals can be found through salvage companies and on-line suppliers, many modern versions are also available. The industrially produced pressed 'milk glass' shade gives a softer spread of light through its opaque and often ribbed white surface. Other ribbed glass shades have a silvered interior surface, which reflects the light and increases its strength. Enamelled steel shades give a less forgiving light, directing the beam directly on the table or worktop below. The upper or outer surface of the shade can be enamelled in a range of colours, such as brown and black, or left as shining silvery steel.

Perhaps the best-known industrial task light is the Anglepoise, a balanced-arm lamp patented in 1933. The Anglepoise was created by George Carwardine, a British car designer specializing in vehicle suspension systems. While developing new concepts for vehicle suspensions, he created a mechanism with multiple joints and spring tension that allowed for easy movement into a wide range of positions that could be maintained without being clamped.

Light & white

RIGHT Mass-produced, stamped metal stools, an industrial rubber floor and a ceramic tile-covered wall create a plain functional space softened only by the introduction of a retro-styled fridge.

BELOW By painting this wooden furniture white it makes it more clinical and work-like; if left in natural wood or painted a primary colour it would be more suitable for a country-style setting.

The original four-spring Anglepoise was regarded as being too industrial for a domestic market, so in 1935 Carwardine, together with manufacturer Herbert Terry and Sons Ltd, developed a three-spring version that is still in production. In the 1970s another industrial designer, Sir Kenneth Grange, developed the Type 75, which transformed the Anglepoise into a wall light. There is also a slim floor-standing version and even a giant floor-standing version, but the original 1227 table-top design, still available in cream, black or red, is the most desirable and sought after.

Wall and floor surfaces in the utilitarian kitchen tend to be plain, never fussy, but with a nod to industrial sources. Melamine, Formica and natural rubber linoleum are all suitable, as are thin sheets or tiles of metal, although for some more 'aged' schemes the newness of the metal may need to be dulled with a patination or weathered effect. This can be done with a mild chemical wash, the light tarnishing produced by a blow torch or a combination of both these techniques. Plain wooden floorboards, left in natural wooden tones or given a protective coat of white paint, whether muted barely there whitewash or more clinical shiny-white high gloss, are always a good option.

Walls may be of bare brick to fit the utilitarian look, but in areas close to where food is being prepared or cooked add a protective seal of matt varnish to protect the brick surface and prevent small particles from falling off onto surfaces or into food. Blackboard paint makes a useful covering for a feature wall, and the space can be used for chalking up recipes for the evening's dinner, shopping lists and the family's weekly agenda. If you opt for painting the walls, try muddy muted shades such as beige, grey or green or simple, no-nonsense white.

THIS PAGE This kitchen has elements of both country and utilitarian styles, but the trio of suspended lights over the stove, the zinc-topped table and scrubbed wooden floor give it just enough workman-like edge to qualify for this style.

Kitchenalia
Elements

Furniture

When it comes to furniture for the *Kitchenalia* kitchen there are four options: restore and repair old pieces; adapt something for a different purpose; artificially 'age' a new piece; or buy a re-edition of an old classic.

Some manufacturers famous for their earlier cutting-edge designs are now reissuing them. For example, Ercol, the company founded by Lucian Ercolani in 1920, is once again producing furniture from that period, as well as the 1950s – currently popular pieces include its Butterfly, Fleur de Lys and classic Windsor chairs.

Although many modern homes have fitted kitchens, freestanding cupboards, butcher's blocks and sometimes repurposed items of furniture can be introduced to break up the uniformity of the room and give it a more individual appearance. Old linen presses or armoires with their deep capacious shelves can make useful store cupboards for china or tinned and dry goods, and a dresser can be concocted from a chest of drawers with a set of open shelves placed on top.

The hardware, in the form of a stove or range, and the sink are also important in achieving this look, and again can be bought old and refurbished, or sourced new. For example, the classic Belfast or butler's sink or an enamelled range can both be found in reclamation yards as well as brand-new on the high street.

ABOVE LEFT Because of the size and proportions of this style of dresser it is often found built into a home, or you can have one made to measure by a competent carpenter.

LEFT Fitted units with doors would have made the area above the sink restricted and dark, while these open display shelves are light and attractive.

RIGHT By replacing the upper wooden panels of a cupboard with panes of glass you can make a solid unit more accessible and less dominant in a room.

Cabinets & drawers

The best way to sum up this section of *Kitchenalia* is to say 'think outside the box'. In this style of room cabinets and drawers don't have to conform to the norm: they can be recycled, up-cycled or reinvented. For example, an old shop fitting, especially a glass-fronted display cabinet, makes a strong and impressive feature in a kitchen. The glass-panelled doors on the upper section allow decorative china and other interesting goods to be protected from the steam and dust while still being on show.

This type of fitting often comes with a lower section of little drawers or niches that would once have been out of sight, below counter level. These containers would have been where ribbons or threads were stored, but now they can be used for knives, forks, spoons, napkins, candles and other smaller items. Vintage museum display cases, library bookcases, chemist's cabinets and even freestanding wardrobes can be adapted to fulfil a useful purpose in a kitchen. They made need to be sanded and revarnished or painted to give them a fresher, cleaner appearance, but as long as the structure is solid they should be easy to adapt. If a piece is very heavy or resting on an uneven floor it is advisable to secure these larger items of furniture to the walls with a couple of sturdy brackets to avoid them toppling over.

LEFT Old shop fittings make good dressers and the recesses that once housed items of haberdashery or gentlemen's attire can be used for storing glasses and china.

BELOW LEFT The original markings on these drawers, from a carpenter's workshop, have been left as a reminder of its original use.

BELOW Make sure that old units, like these wooden drawers, are well scrubbed and checked for woodworm before you bring them into the kitchen.

If you don't have one single unit or cupboard, or the space to accommodate a larger piece of furniture, you can concoct your own dresser or cabinet out of two separate sections. For the lower piece a standard chest of drawers, even one originally destined for a bedroom, will do. Then above arrange a set of open shelves – again something that might have been used in a study or sitting room will work well. The shelves can be secured directly to the wall while the cupboard remains freestanding.

You may already have fitted cabinets in your kitchen, especially if you live in a modern house or apartment. In this case, you may be able to change the doors to something more *Kitchenalia* style or adapt them yourself by adding a panel of plywood, which can be painted to suit your scheme, or a facing of laminate such as Formica.

Drawers are very useful in a kitchen, especially small ones where a single type of object can be stored. For example, a drawer for paper table napkins, another for cotton or linen napkins and another for tablemats. This makes it easier to identify and find things, rather than hunting through a stack of various linens stored in a single large drawer.

Again drawers can be recycled, for example from a hardware-store fitting where the individual sections were used to keep certain sizes of screws or types of drill bits. Drawers don't have to come fitted in a unit – the same type of storage can be obtained by arranging wooden boxes on suitably deep shelves. The boxes can be old wine crates or packing cases, and you can either add a conventional handle to the front or make an appropriate grab handle from a length of attractive rope or cord slipped through two suitably positioned and drilled holes.

FAR LEFT Wooden furniture is versatile; if it's painted you could strip it back to the wood or if it is a plain wood, paint it to blend with a wall colour or fabric in the room.

LEFT The interior of the cabinet is painted white as a fresh uncomplicated backdrop to the items stored and displayed inside while the doors, painted in a dark colour, act as frames.

Glass-fronted cabinets create a point of interest as well as providing dust and grease-free storage.

THIS PAGE The 1950s aluminium English Rose kitchen was developed by CSA Industries, a company that had previously made nose cones for Spitfires during World War II.

RIGHT Plain unit doors can be painted in bold colours or faced with Formica to create a vintage look.

ABOVE Ventilated metal kit lockers, usually found in schools or workplaces, are often recycled as a useful storage cabinet for pots and pans or tins and packets of foods.

Furniture   123

CHOOSING CABINETS

✦ Replace the solid or damaged wooden panels in the centre of a cupboard door with toughened glass, chicken wire or pleated fabric for a fresher, brighter look.

✦ When buying an old wooden unit or cupboard check for signs of rot or woodworm. If in any doubt treat with a branded or recommended product before bringing the piece into your home.

✦ Old windows can be recycled as cupboard doors. Their weathered appearance may be attractive but if the paint is peeling you should secure it by removing the loose pieces with sandpaper or a stiff wire brush, and then seal with a coat of clear varnish to make it hygienic and viable for kitchen use.

✦ Make a plain modern door unit more interesting by adding an inner surround of beading or a paint effect such as a grainy colourwash.

✦ Replacing handles and knobs is a quick and inexpensive way of giving a plain modern unit a more dated look or making a feature of a plain pine or wood cupboard.

LEFT If putting together separate pieces of furniture to create your own dresser make sure that the proportions are balanced and pleasing to the eye.

RIGHT, CLOCKWISE FROM TOP LEFT The original bow-fronted drawer with recessed handles and aluminium back plate on a classic English Rose kitchen unit.

A dresser-style effect has been made in this corner by placing a wall-mounted cabinet above a freestanding cupboard.

For an interesting chance of pace, paint or paper the inside of a cupboard or shelves with a contrasting colour.

If you have a collection of chinaware or different kitchenalia, paint your cupboard a colour that will enhance its display.

Butcher's blocks

Butcher's blocks could, in the broadest terms, also be termed shop fittings because they were the heavy-duty wooden chopping blocks or boards on which a butcher cut and trimmed meat to size or to fulfil a specific order. These blocks are traditionally made from end-grain sections because this angle of the wood grain was more stable and more able to withstand the force and pressure of the butcher's heavy blades. Blocks made with face grain, where the wood lies horizontal, tend to be less resilient and show cut marks and dents more clearly. Modern versions of butcher's blocks are often mounted on lockable wheels and made from offcuts of wooden worktops, so may be constructed from acacia, rock maple or other hardwoods.

Genuine, old blocks are often worn away in areas where the butcher most frequently worked, and where the wood was sanded back to clean it, so they have a curve or hollow. As they were used in shops they are also quite large, many the size of a table top, which in a contemporary home would provide a serviceable worktop area.

ABOVE LEFT This butcher's block fits neatly within the frame of the wide window.

ABOVE You may need to have a base custom-made to raise the block to a comfortable kitchen worktop height.

RIGHT A small wooden block mounted on wheels provides a movable chopping area, with useful extra storage underneath for pots and pans.

Mobile & freestanding furniture

Mobile units are useful in both large and small kitchens. In a large kitchen a unit on wheels can be brought into the work triangle (the area of main activity between the sink, hob and fridge) to reduce the amount of walking from one point to the other by providing an extra area of worktop. In a small kitchen the mobile unit can be incorporated into the work triangle, but moved back against the wall or out of the way when more central space is required.

Trolleys are practical because they can be used to transport things from one side of a room to another or from one room to the next, and they also double as a storage area. Freestanding furniture, which isn't attached to the wall, is beneficial if you have an area of plasterboard or a non-supporting wall to which units cannot be secured; you can position units against it, rather than hanging them for the wall.

Freestanding furniture also allows for seasonal changes. For example, you may slide or wheel a unit in front of a garden door during the winter, but move it in the summer when you want to have access to the garden. Also, if you plan to move to a new home, it is easy to pack up and transport a freestanding unit, whereas a secured piece would be counted as a fixture and fitting and left behind.

FAR LEFT A lightweight trolley is ideal for transporting drinks or dishes from one room to another.

CENTRE LEFT This stout metal trolley had an industrial heritage, but now provides useful extra kitchen storage.

LEFT Probably plain wood to begin with, this unit has been transformed with blue paint and positioned against a panel of decorative tiles.

ABOVE A hanging rack is a useful piece in any kitchen, providing extra storage in a dead space area. This one is set above a block set into a run of units and worktop to provide a useful break in uniformity.

Tables & chairs

Some people like round tables because you are more accessible and visible to those sitting around it. Others prefer the formality of a rectangular table, although it restricts conversation to those on either side or immediately across from you, but for most of us it is more often about what fits into the available space than social convention.

In a small room a round or square table will probably allow more usable space, whereas in a long, narrow kitchen a rectangular table can be arranged to run parallel with the walls, leaving corridors of space of either side. In a kitchen–dining area the table may double as an additional worktop, so the height and surface are important, although a plasticized or PVC-coated cloth could be used to protect the table top. If you are tall and the table low you may get backache from standing and leaning over, so have an adjustable stool that allows you to sit and work comfortably at the table.

The gate-leg table, dating from the sixteenth century, traditionally has side panels that can be lifted and secured or folded down below the fixed section to hang vertically. This type of table is ideal for a small kitchen because its size can be adapted to suit various needs and functions. When folded it can still provide a useful perch for an early-morning cup of coffee. Then when all the family gather it can be opened out for meals. Even in a larger kitchen a gate-leg is a useful second table that can be pushed

ABOVE LEFT A mix-and-match selection of elegant period chairs are brought together by being painted the same shade of grey.

ABOVE Where there isn't space for single chairs, a small bench may be a better option.

RIGHT Chair design is often representative of its time; these vinyl-upholstered metal-framed seats evoke a real 1950s feel.

up against a wall in its folded state. When needed for entertaining it can be brought out to sit alongside the main dining table with one or two of the leaves elevated and secured, to flexibly accommodate larger groups.

Because of its versatility the gate-leg table has been continually made, in one form or another, throughout the centuries, so there are many in second-hand shops and sales. The traditional dark-stained oak version may look a little heavy for modern tastes. But if the wood is good and the structure sound, it can still be a useful piece of furniture. It will just need some cleaning and sanding to take it back to a paler shade of natural wood or to prepare it for a colourful coat of paint.

Chairs, especially in a kitchen–dining area, need to be comfortable. Traditional styles such as the Windsor are still manufactured, although the design can be traced back to the 1600s. The Windsor chair has a solid wooden seat with drilled holes into which the chair-back and legs are secured (in other chairs the back legs and uprights of the back are usually continuous pieces of wood). The seats of Windsor chairs generally have a

BELOW Windsor chairs with solid seats and back spindles and legs set into drilled holes in the seat are a classic design often found in country-style kitchens.

RIGHT These Thonet-style bentwood chairs with cane seats are elegantly curvacious and lightweight, and would suit almost any formal table design.

shallow dish or saddle-shape seat, and the spokes at the back, and sometimes the arms if they are present, are made from turned spindles that are thought to have come from the spokes once made by wheelwrights. The basic design is found in many parts of the world, including Wales and the West Country of England; in Ireland they are referred to as 'stick-back' chairs.

Many contemporary designs work well in the *Kitchenalia* kitchen. For example, Robin Day's 675 chairs, first produced in the 1960s, are still in production, as are the works of Florence Knoll, co-founder of the Knoll brand. She described her designs as 'the meat and potatoes, the fill-in pieces which had to be provided' yet her slimline marble-topped oval table is still popular today.

And as well as the permanent chairs around your table it can be useful to have a couple of foldaway types that can be kept in a cupboard or hung out of the way on a peg rail. If they are metal or plastic have a couple of cushion pads to make them more comfortable when in use.

LEFT Industrial-style metal chairs are sturdy and robust, but can be made more comfortable with the addition of a seat cushion.

ABOVE Bentwood chairs with black lacquer frames and rattan seats have a certain amount of 'give' and support, which makes them comfortable to sit on for a long leisurely meal.

RIGHT With traditional Mediterranean-style country chairs the woodwork is often painted green or lavender, as are the wooden window shutters of the houses in these regions.

Shelving & china display

When displaying china, grouping is important. There is the classic guideline that odd numbered groups are more interesting to the eye. With long shelves and a variety of china you might try putting the tallest item in the middle then, on either side, grading the other pieces down in size. Layering is another option; put patterned plates upright at the back of the shelf, then small bowls or jugs in front. Positioning can also have an effect. For example, plain plates with a scalloped edged will look best stacked at eye level so that the decorative border is on view rather than the plain, uninteresting surface. Alternatively, arrange them vertically so their shape can be appreciated.

Grouping like things together can double their impact: a whole dresser of blue-and-white willowware will be eye-catching, as will a collection of cow creamer jugs lined up nose to tail. Even fairly ordinary everyday objects can be brought into play – a bunch of Brown Betty teapots make more of an impression than one on its own.

Glassware on display must be clean and sparkling; those that are cloudy from the dishwasher or plain workaday objects should be kept behind closed doors. Glasses, because of their lightness and transparency, can be used to create a break or 'pause' between groups of heavier or more patterned items on a shelf.

LEFT This walk-in pantry, as may be found in large houses and stately homes, gives ample space to store dinner services and tea sets as well as cooking bowls, wine and baskets, while cupboards in the kitchen itself may be used to store everyday tableware and foodstuff.

RIGHT In this small kitchen a set of open shelves provides an area of attractive storage. It has been positioned high up the wall to avoid interfering with access to the stove or damage from its heat.

If you are making your own shelving you could graduate the size, so that you have narrower shelves at the bottom for smaller items and wider ones at the top for bigger dishes and jugs. The batons, brackets or corbels that support the shelves can also contribute to the appearance, so choose them carefully. For example, earthenware pots will be in keeping with plain wooden shelves supported by half-circle wooden brackets. Black, wrought-iron scroll brackets will suit a glass shelf of 1950s-style china, while an ornate Victorian-style acanthus-design bracket would be in keeping with a lace-edged shelf supporting a Wedgwood tea service. Alternatively, a 'floating' shelf, with invisible fixings to attach it to the wall, is a neutral framework on which all manner and styles of china collections can be stored and displayed.

ABOVE Where space is limited rows of cup hooks can be used under shelves to maximize what is available by keeping cups and mugs in place.

RIGHT Arrange shelves so that things used every day, such as cups and mugs, are at the lower level and readily accessible, with serving vessels positioned higher up.

FAR RIGHT This fine ornate shelving system not only looks attractive, but is also useful for keeping lightweight objects, such as glasses, in order.

Plate racks

Plate racks come in various shapes and sizes, from the small folding type that can be used on a draining board beside a sink, to a wall-mounted piece of cabinetry. The thing they all have in common is that they store plates, and sometimes pots and pans, by means of wooden or metal batons or struts.

Racks can be purpose-built or adapted from other pieces of furniture. For example, a set of widely spaced bookshelves could be divided with lengths of dowel fixed into holes drilled in the top and bottom of the shelves. Sections of baton could also be secured across a door to make a rack for large serving plates and platters. Ornate trimmings and finishes can be added to increase the importance of the piece; scalloped side panels and a pelmet-like top will enhance its stature and prestige as part of the room's decorative scheme. Plate racks can be painted or the wood can be left plain. Painted ones tend to have horizontal batons and are decorated to either blend in with the colour of the wall against which it is positioned, or in contrast.

ABOVE LEFT This plate rack holds tableware that is in regular use, while the shelves are more for display and contain decorative and vintage china. Rows of hooks hold cups and utensils.

ABOVE A small wooden drying rack may not only hold plates, but the end can also be fitted with hooks to accommodate brushes and sieves.

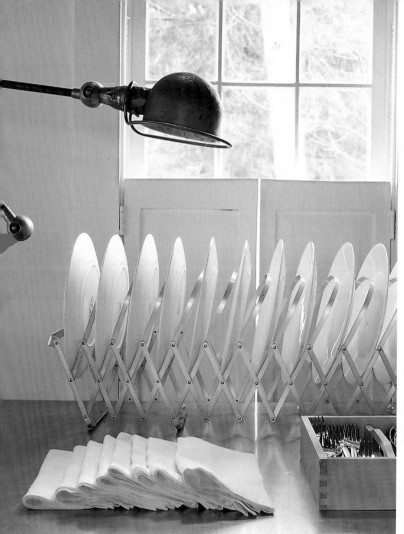

ABOVE If you are entertaining a large number of people and can't readily accommodate the quantity of plates required then an extendable dish rack like this one is ideal as a temporary fix.

ABOVE RIGHT Plate racks are often positioned above the sink so that excess water from freshly washed plates can drip back into the bowl beneath.

Plate racks need to be robust and firmly attached to the wall – the total weight of a dozen dinner plates, assorted dishes and serving platters soon mounts up.

Sometimes a colour is chosen to highlight the collection of china being stored and displayed. For example, if the wall behind the dresser is blue, and the china to be kept on the plate rack is a collection of blue-and-white willowware, then the rack could be painted white to create a break between the wall and china colours.

Plain wooden racks tend to be utilitarian and workman-like, with vertical struts so that the plates are stacked upright for optimum space efficiency, and placed over a sink or worktop. Wood has a natural antiseptic quality, which makes it a good material for storing plates that may be damp or draining.

LEFT Narrow, lateral plate racks are ideal for storing larger platters and serving dishes, which if stacked horizontally on shelves would be space consuming and difficult to access.

RIGHT The inside panels of a pair of double doors act as storage for the larger pieces of a dinner service. When closed, the doors face the kitchen; when open they face the dining room.

Hidden storage

There is always equipment in a kitchen that is essential but unattractive, so better not seen, and food items whose packaging does the job but doesn't contribute anything visually. For these areas and objects the cupboard was invented and where you don't have a cupboard a useful concealing curtain will hide them from view.

Curtains are an effective way to hide shelves and can be easily hung from a length of bamboo pole, a broom handle or a few metres of plastic-coated wiring fixed or set into a cup hook at either end. The curtains don't have to be made from material. They can be fabricated from fine woven grass matting cut to size, vinyl fringe, even, in certain areas such as a utility room or pantry, shower curtains. If the length of material required is small it can be a great place to use a piece of vintage fabric bought as a one-off piece, or for an expensive fabric of which you can only afford a limited amount.

The advantage of curtains is that they can be used in a small or narrow area where there isn't enough space to open a hinged door. Standard unit and cupboard doors require floor space equivalent to their size to open and fully access what is inside, but with a curtain you can simply pull it to one side or flip it back over the surface above and you have a clear and unobstructed view of the shelves and contents behind.

The one disadvantage of curtain-covered storage is that dust and insects have almost unrestricted access, so it is important to regularly pull back the curtains and brush the area thoroughly. Clean the back of the shelves where the dark, warm crannies may invite small creatures to set up home.

Curtains can be simply hung by means of a plastic-coated wire run through a tube of fabric sewn at the top, or by inserting eyelets through which a piece of wooden dowel can be threaded.

FAR LEFT Another set of white doors, like those of the units on the upper part of the adjacent wall, could have made this room bland, whereas the curtains add pattern and colour.

LEFT This small check-patterned curtain acts as a transition between the solid wall colour and the dominant blue-and-white floor tiles.

STORAGE ON DISPLAY

✦ Storage should be arranged so that the contents are close to the area where they will be used. Tableware needs to be located near the table or sink and dishwasher; pots and pans close to the hob and stove; teacups and coffee mugs beside the kettle.

✦ Storage on open shelves can be supplemented with a row of butcher's hooks suspended from a rail, or cup hooks screwed and secured to the underside of the shelves. A Shaker peg rail is also handy for tea towels, brushes and even large jugs.

✦ Line a shelf with offcuts of wallpaper or decorative wrapping paper. Not only will it add colour and pattern, but it will also make surface less damaging to the rims of upturned china cups and delicate glassware.

✦ The edge of a plain or blunt-cut shelf can be given an attractive appearance with a trimming of cut paper, lace or ribbon.

✦ China can be heavier than you think. Be careful when putting stacks of plates on a shelf; their combined weight may cause the shelf to buckle or break. Either spread the load in several smaller piles or add additional supports or struts beneath the shelf.

LEFT Industrial shelving, fitted into a narrow space under a sloping ceiling, provides open storage for pots and pans as well as dried and tinned foods.

RIGHT, CLOCKWISE FROM TOP LEFT Attractively patterned tin canisters and biscuit boxes make an appealing colourful display on modern steel-edged shelves.

An old soft drinks crate, complete with name check, has been recycled as a small but attractive cup store.

A metal shelf supports storage jars and containers above, as well as an array of utensils suspended below.

A plain shelf is given a face-lift with cotton lace. This could be attached with Velcro so that it can be removed for washing to keep it pristine.

Surfaces

Many types of surface coverings are interchangeable between walls, floors and worktops. Natural materials, such as wood and stone, can be used in thin veneers or planks for most areas, as can clay and glazed ceramic tiles.

Man-made finishes come in many forms, but for some their historical designs influence their modern products. For example, Formica, the manufacturer of high pressure laminate, is over 100 years old and although it produces many contemporary designs, it still has a number with vintage roots that reflect its heritage.

Lino, or to give it its full name linoleum, has been around since the 1850s when Frederick Walton invented it while looking for a more resilient alternative to the painted oilcloth. Lino is now popular not only because of its composition of natural and renewable materials – including linseed oil, pine resin, cork, wood flour and minerals spread on a burlap or canvas backing – but also because it is hard-wearing and easy to clean.

Vinyl flooring, especially in tile form, can be used to create chequerboard and other geometric patterns. Many manufacturers also offer a laser cutting service to provide decorative borders and motifs for a personalized design. Paint and varnish may also be used to create durable decorative floor finishes.

Metals such as zinc and copper are more often found as coverings for cooker hoods, table tops and sometimes as splashbacks or protective panels behind a stove or hob.

LEFT Ceramic tiles, both patterned and plain, are still a popular surface covering in kitchens, especially with those following a vintage or country-style scheme.

RIGHT This substantial Scottish baronial-style table base was given a new lease of life as an impressive kitchen island by the addition of a new solid wood worktop.

BELOW This worktop is made from a large piece of wood with the original raw edge left in its natural state, rather than planed and sanded to a straight line.

ABOVE Formica, melamine and even lino can be used as a colourful and resilient surface on unit worktops.

RIGHT Poured concrete makes a robust work surface and can be poured on site to fit any awkward shape or situation.

FAR RIGHT Running the worktop up the wall to form a small, integral splashback makes it easy to clean. If this can't be achieved with a single piece of material then join the two separate sections with a sealant.

Worktops

The priority for a worktop is that is should be hard-wearing and easy to clean, so that it is always hygienic. It is possible to use old work surfaces or incorporate parts of recycled materials into a worktop, but they need to be in excellent condition and may require treatment with a steam cleaner or high-pressure water hose before you use them. Recycled materials – such as the thick wooden top from a disused laboratory workbench or a slab of marble from an old dairy counter, or even a bath's marble side panel removed during a hotel refurbishment – can all be given a new life as a section of worktop.

The *Kitchenalia* kitchen doesn't conform to hard-and-fast rules so you can mix and match work surfaces; this not only makes the space more interesting, but it can have practical advantages too. You could have a specific area of marble surface for making pastry, which is best prepared and rolled on a cold surface, or for filleting fish, which also benefits from being kept cool. In another area you could have a section of wooden worktop, ideal for chopping vegetables or cutting bread. On either side of the stove or hob aim to have a surface that is heat resistant or, if you have wood or other material vulnerable to scorch marks, add a protective metal trivet or grille so that hot roasting dishes or baking trays can be laid down speedily and easily without causing damage to the surface.

Stainless steel and zinc are both popular heat-resistant worktop coverings, but they are prone to scratch marks. These can sometimes be softened by polishing with a cloth and oil, but in time they become part of the patina of the surface and soften what can be a rather hard shine on a new steel finish.

Poured concrete is another useful worktop material, and because it is made on site it can be tailor-made to fit irregular or difficult spaces. Some designs are finished with rounded edges, which make it less likely that you will bruise yourself if you bump into a corner and also easier to stretch or lean over. This very contemporary material works best alongside other robust, perhaps reclaimed materials, or within a utilitarian-style kitchen with an industrial feel.

More recently developed acrylic polymer materials such as Corian are very modern, but are adaptable enough to be given a retro feel. They come in a wide range of colours, which can look fun in a 1950s or 60s-style kitchen, as well as grained and stone-like effects. These materials can also be seamlessly joined, which makes them easy to clean, and the shapes can be curved for a softer more ergonomic design. Unlike marble or granite, which are cold and hard, Corian is warm to the touch.

BELOW LEFT In a small galley or corridor kitchen matching parallel work surfaces can be a good way to optimize the available space.

BELOW Zinc was traditionally used as a covering in work areas because when heated it is malleable and can be beaten or hammered into shape. It also has an anti-corrosive element, used in the galvanization of iron and steel, so it is resilient to water.

LEFT Polished stone has a luxurious appearance and makes a hard-wearing, waterproof worktop, especially suited to use in wet areas around the sink.

ABOVE This worktop has been made by wrapping a thin sheet of zinc around a wooden form or template. It is then secured in place with small, flat-top nails hammered into the edge.

Walls & splashbacks

Many of the materials used for worktops can also be used for splashbacks and wall coverings – in fact marble, Corian, steel and zinc are often carried through so that there is an almost seamless run from horizontal to vertical surfaces.

Since the advent of toughened glass this easy-to-clean transparent material has become popular for splashbacks. It can be produced in long lengths, so avoiding the nooks and crannies of traditional tiling and the areas of grout that often become greasy and stained. The back of the glass can also be coloured or painted so that it is a part of the overall decorative scheme.

Ceramic tiles have long been used in kitchens because their shiny, glazed surface is hard-wearing and resilient. These tiles come in many styles and shapes. Currently popular is the Metro tile: a brick-like oblong shape like those found on the walls of the Parisian underground. They are mainly available in plain colours and give a utilitarian appearance.

Perennially popular are small, square-patterned ceramic tiles. These can be handmade, which makes them more expensive, or factory-made, with slightly irregular surfaces and a mottled coloured glaze, so that they appear handmade. You can also pick up vintage tiles in second-hand shops and car boot sales; these can be gathered together to create a patchwork-like panel that will be a focal point in an otherwise plain kitchen.

FAR LEFT A panel of wood painted with blackboard paint makes a hard-wearing and useful splashback behind the cooker on this end return.

LEFT Ceramic tiles can withstand heat and splashes of hot oil from the hob, but from time to time the grout may need to be raked out and replaced.

ABOVE Reinforced glass is popular as a splashback because it is easy to wipe clean and protects the wall.

If you are thinking of making a panel of vintage tiles, try to stick to a theme or palette of colours to achieve visual cohesion. It is also important that the wall to which you are going to attach them is level – if you try to straighten a tile on an uneven wall it will crack. Also if the tiles have been salvaged you will need to carefully chip off and clean the back of any residue adhesive so that they will lie perfectly flat and evenly on the wall.

You can just leave the walls plain and painted or sealed. If you opt for paint look at vinyl emulsions, because they are washable and will provide a degree of protection to porous plaster or wood. Plain plaster walls should be sealed with a clear matt varnish when they are thoroughly dry, and in areas where the wall surface is uneven or likely to be bumped and battered, wooden tongue-and-groove panelling can provide an attractive and sturdy covering.

ABOVE LEFT An upstand of stainless steel provides resilient and easy-to-clean wall protection and complements the worktop.

LEFT Tongue-and-groove panelling painted to contrast with the walls helps to create a more intimate feeling in this large room with a high ceiling.

RIGHT A variety of patterned decorative ceramic tiles make an eye-catching splashback to an old stone sink.

Floors

In a small, dark kitchen try a pale coloured floor to reflect any available light and give the room a brighter, less cramped feel; in a big kitchen you could go for something with a bold pattern or a rich, dark colour, but beware of the practical aspects. Plain dark grey or black flooring may look grand and dramatic but it will also show up every spill mark, grain of flour and crumb, so be prepared for regular brushing and cleaning.

In a large kitchen–dining room you could also divide the flooring so that in the dining area you have wood or stone flags, while between the island and sink, or in the area where the work triangle is focused, you have an area of vinyl tiles or lino that are resilient to hot and cold spills and easy to clean.

LEFT Aged bricks and clay tiles are a suitable floor covering for country-style kitchens and can be left matt or polished with wax to a shiny finish.

ABOVE Untreated terracotta tiles are brittle so need to be laid on a completely level surface or they may crack and break. Traditionally, they were set on earth or sand.

RIGHT Flagstone floors have been used in homes for centuries, but modern versions are available in lighter composite or artificial stone, which comes in a range of textures and colours.

If you choose to have stone or wood throughout you could lay a length of rubber matting in the preparation and cooking zone, so that it will catch grease, drips and crumbs, but can be taken outside and shaked, then hosed down for a thorough clean, or simply brushed and washed in situ.

If you have an old wooden floor you can revive it by sanding off any seal or varnish and putting on a fresh coat that will bring back its richness and shine. For a change, you could stain the wood a different colour before reapplying the varnish.

Those of an artistic disposition could try making a stencil and painting or staining a pattern onto the wood, such as a border motif or even faux tile pattern. If the surface is battered from use or the wood itself is a dull and interesting type, then you could simply paint over or lime-wash it to give a lighter, almost weather-beaten appearance.

ABOVE RIGHT A plain white painted wood floor looks immaculate when new, but needs to be washed regularly to maintain its appearance.

RIGHT Patterns can be stencilled or painted onto wooden floors to liven up specific areas. To protect the surface it is best to seal with a clear varnish when finished.

FAR RIGHT Wood stain and dye are alternatives to painting wooden floors, and give a softer finish that allow the grain to show through.

OPPOSITE A light wood floor will reflect the daylight and give a room a bright open appearance. Pale wood floors such as those made from pine or ash need to be sealed or protected with wax or varnish.

LEFT Ceramic tiles can be used as a floor covering but are prone to crack and chip, whereas patterned lino, which can be bought in large rolls, is more resilient.

BELOW A subtle rustic take on the traditional black-and white chequerboard flooring, is this combination of smaller cream-and-terracotta tiles.

RIGHT The perennially popular black-and-white chequerboard floor is a classic background that works in many styles of kitchen.

Among the most durable flooring materials is stone, but due to its weight you need to be careful when installing it in a large room on an upper level. A couple of dozen flagstones will add up to a considerable weight and may cause a floor supported by wooden beams to sag, so do take advice from a structural engineer before laying a stone floor in an upstairs room.

Vinyl and linoleum are the most versatile and colourful of the floor coverings. These manmade materials can be printed to look like marble, stone or metal, or even a pebble-covered beach or a grassy lawn; they can be produced in a myriad of colours, or plain or densely patterned, and laid in tile form or cut from a large roll. In a room where you might like a stone floor, but fear that the weight and expense might be too much, you can achieve the look of stone with a good-quality tile or lino.

Another floor covering that is worth considering for a kitchen is rubber. Widely used in industrial sites and commercial settings such as gyms and swimming pools, textured rubber flooring has become popular in contemporary homes. There are many styles and colours to choose from and some of the primary-coloured examples have a strong 1950s and 60s appearance that makes them suitable for a *Kitchenalia*-style kitchen.

Lighting

An important part of a kitchen, lighting and can be divided into two types: task, which illuminates work surfaces and areas where cooking takes place, and decorative.

Decorative lighting can add to the ambient or background light, as well as the mood and appearance of a room. For a kitchen and dining area you could have fun using recycled colanders or jelly moulds as shades. Light will spill through the holes in the colander and make patterns on the walls and ceiling, while a copper jelly mound will give the reflected beams a warm, rosy pink hue. In a small and steamy kitchen enclosed mounted shades for the wall or ceiling can be advantageous, and these can be found in ships chandlers and other nautical suppliers.

Task lighting is also a safety feature and should provide clear and directional illumination so that you can see clearly in areas where sharp knives and hot pans will be in use.

Wiring and electrical connections for recycled and vintage lighting must be done by a professional, but to carry the vintage-style finish through you may want to source fabric-covered light cable. Twisted braid-style cable comes in a range of colours, from bright red to gold, and can be the perfect finishing touch to a light.

ABOVE LEFT An old industrial metal light makes a dramatic focus on a breakfast bar and adds a vintage note to the scheme in a modern fitted kitchen, also picked up in the wall clock and retro chrome and leather stools.

RIGHT By mixing the shapes and heights of these gilt shades the lighting becomes an important part of the look of the room and attracts attention to this area.

Lighting is an important part of any kitchen but more so in the *Kitchenalia* kitchen because it not only provides focused illumination on worktops, but also plays an important role in setting the mood and style of the room.

The practical target of task lighting that is focused on the work surface should always be clear, straightforward and effective. Most of this type of lighting can be provided by modern strip or LED devices concealed under the base of an overhead unit. Where it is visible, task lighting should follow the style of the rest of the room, so an adjustable wall-mounted lamp is ideal, or a series of evenly spaced lights that give a clear wash of light over the worktop. But be careful to arrange these so that the light shines in front of you; if the beam shines from behind you your body will cast a shadow over the area at which you are working and the light won't serve its purpose.

Modern versions of vintage-style work lights are available, as are contemporary industrial fittings such as bulb guards and cages and die-cast aluminium bar lights, which have a practical, no-nonsense appearance – perfect for the utilitarian look. These new lights will have the correct fittings and fixtures to comply with current safety standards and be certified safe to use in high-risk areas, such as the kitchen, where a lethal mix of water and electricity is ever present.

BELOW LEFT Inverted enamelled funnels make unexpected shades, but pick up on the quirky decorative theme indicated by the rough paint finish on the walls.

BELOW Old fittings come in a range of shapes, as demonstrated in the variety on display in this kitchen. It may be necessary to rewire old light fittings, especially if sourced from another country, to ensure that they are made safe and compatible.

RIGHT Adjustable work lights, usually found on an office desk, have been adapted to create a fun trio of lights over an island work station.

LEFT This paper lampshade will create a soft diffuse light over the table, while the light emitted from the holes on the side will be a bright beam.

RIGHT This elaborate chandelier complements the ornate panelling and decorative mirror also seen in this room, but will provide a useful amount of light.

As well as task lighting, you should aim to focus light on certain areas of the room, such as breakfast bar or island unit, and around a dining table. This type of lighting can be used to define spaces in a larger room and, if wired to dimmer switches, can be used to isolate or highlight one particular zone. For example, you can dim or turn off the light in the kitchen once the food has been served so that the focus of attention is away from the dirty dishes and onto the dining area.

Many streamlined modern kitchens opt for almost invisible recessed ceiling lights or a bank of anonymous directional spots, but in the *Kitchenalia* kitchen lights are bold and there to be noticed. Whether they have vintage shades or are reappropriated industrial fittings, they will make their mark.

A ceiling light will contribute to the overall illumination of the kitchen, but it can also be a decorative feature, picking up on a colour, style or period.

There is a whole area of inventive lighting that uses recycled kitchenware. These items not only look at home in this space, but they are usually robust because they have withstood years of high-temperature baking. Colanders, jelly moulds, fruit bottling jars and enamel funnels can all be adapted.

There are vintage lights that are appropriate to a certain style or era, and some that are classic and fit in with a wide range of styles. Colourful Venini glass shades look dramatic and can be chosen to pick up on a particular colour scheme. The coloured glass tints the light that shines through it, so an orange shade will give the light a warm and mellow appearance while a blue shade will make it moody and cool.

Many classic light shades, such as George Nelson's Bubble lamp, designed in 1947, and Poul Henningsen's Snowball and Artichoke, are statement pieces, designed to be hung in isolation as pendant or ceiling lights.

Another classic statement piece is the chandelier, and even though this book is about kitchen styling, there are no rules to say that you can't go grand and have a twinkle of sparkling glass. But if you don't have the height or space for a chandelier, why not create a similar effect by bunching together a group of similar-style lights to create a cluster. With this amount of volume, don't forget to lower the wattage of the bulbs so that you aren't dazzled by the glare of a multitude of lights.

THIS PAGE This enamel nautical light could be new or a well-maintained vintage version. The style is classic and will provide a good level of light, whether used indoors or out.

LEFT The light emitted through the sides of this glass shade will be tinted blue, while the beam directed onto the table top will be bright white.

LET THERE BE LIGHT

❦ In areas of the kitchen where steam and grease accumulate it is best to avoid fabric and fabric-lined shades because they will absorb moisture and over time the fabric will become limp and stained.

❦ Make your own unique chandelier by hanging old crystal earrings and broken bits of necklace as well as miscellaneous glass drops from a lampshade frame. Use fine wire, such as is found in florists' shops or fly-fishing outlets, to attach the glass. The wire is strong yet almost invisible and will enable you to construct a more ordered arrangement.

❦ Small glass yoghurt pots can be used to make decorative lights. Wrap a circle of fine wire securely around the neck of the pot, leaving a length at the beginning and end so that the pot can be suspended from and attached to the frame. Once you have assembled the requisite number of pots, fill them with tea lights.

❦ Suspend old silver forks and spoons with decorative handles from a metal frame around a light and the heat will make them twist and turn, catching the light and adding sparkle and interest to your table.

LEFT A frosted ribbed glass shade is an anonymous source of light, allowing the collection of bright kitchenware to be the focus of attention.

RIGHT, CLOCKWISE FROM TOP LEFT Adjustable work lights can be turned and twisted to focus the beam directly onto the work area or to bounce light off the wall for a subtle dining-style illumination.

A bunch of vintage glass lampshades suspended close together becomes a colourful and decorative feature.

Chandeliers can be densely or randomly decorated to suit the size and style of your kitchen.

Basketwork shades add a rustic touch, and light shining through the open weave will create patterns on the walls and ceiling.

Pots & Pans

The pots and pans in the *Kitchenalia* kitchen will inevitably be a mix of old and new, and in varying conditions, which in turn may be subdivided into 'show' and 'no-show' when it comes to their arranging and displaying.

ABOVE Copper pans, hung in decreasing size towards the stove, not only look attractive and are an integral part of the style of the kitchen, but are also adjacent to the area where they will be used.

ABOVE RIGHT The spikes on which wine bottles were once dried neck down are now used to suspend pots and lids.

The old will include colourful enamel baking dishes and handsome copper pans while the new will focus on the more technologically advanced equipment that on a day-to-day basis is easy to use and clean. With heat-conducting materials, non-stick finishes and heatproof glass lids that allow us to watch the contents as they bubble and boil, the new kitchen hardware takes much of the guesswork and toil out of cooking, so can't be dismissed. The different shapes and sizes, from roasting tray to wok, and cast-iron casserole to copper sauté pan, need to be arranged so that they make the most economic use of the storage space, and they should also be kept in order of use so that a medium-size saucepan that is employed for a wide variety of tasks, is readily to hand while the fish kettle or cast-iron griddle, which are only occasionally used, may be kept in an upper level cupboard or at the back of a drawer.

THIS PAGE A variety of pans are hung from a ceiling rack carefully positioned over a table so they are out of the way of people's heads when they walk around the room.

FAR LEFT Old copper pans can be found in second-hand shops and car boot sales and are relatively inexpensive, but do require regular maintenance and polishing to keep them clean and shining.

LEFT Copper pans have been used in professional kitchens for centuries; even if you don't use them every day they still make an attractive decorative detail when grouped on a wall.

Pots and pans come with a lot of history and like many designs and furnishings mentioned in this book, the classic styles tend to last, some with a little adaptation and reference to the modern home. Others just stay as they are because they are good at the job they were designed for. The sort of cookware you use may be dictated by the type of oven or stove you have. An easily adjustable gas flame works well with heat-efficient copper pans while cast-iron casseroles and heavy-based pans are ideal for long, slow cooking in an Aga or range.

Among the classic pots and pans are those made of copper, some of which can be picked up in second-hand shops or in sales. The copper pan was originally found in the kitchen of professional French chefs, and companies such as Mauviel have been producing them since 1830. More recently, copper pans are being made with a stainless-steel element to make them more suitable for domestic use; companies such as Falk produce a contemporary bi-metal range.

The *cocotte* or cast-iron casserole is another classic, and perhaps the best known of all is Le Creuset. These pots have a coloured exterior and a smooth creamy enamelled interior. One of the iconic colours for the outer glaze is volcanic orange, and although associated strongly with the 1960s and its introduction into Terence Conran's Habitat chain in the UK, the colour was first produced in 1925 when the Le Creuset factory opened.

Another classic of the kitchen is Pyrex, the borosilicate glass developed in the 1880s that by 1911 was being used for the manufacture of casseroles and dishes. It can be used in ovens up to temperatures of 300°C (572°F), as well as sent through the dishwasher, plonked in the freezer or zapped in the microwave. With its transparent appearance and classic simple styling it still fits into any style of kitchen.

COOKING ESSENTIALS

❧ By hanging pots and pans from hooks you will prevent the inside surfaces, such as enamel or non-stick, from becoming scratched by the base of a pan that might otherwise be stacked on top.

❧ If you do have to stack pots and pans turn the lid of the lower pot upside down so that it seals the lower pots and provides a level base on which the one above can be stacked.

❧ Where space is restricted hang pots from a length of stout chain secured to the ceiling, so that they are stored vertically rather than horizontally.

❧ Classic pots and pans, especially the polished copper variety, can be hung on the wall or above a range or hob as part of the overall kitchen decoration. This also allows warm air to circulate and dry them, which will prevent any residual washing up water from corroding or damaging the surface.

❧ Some modern copper pans look like the vintage variety but have a clear varnish to protect the outer surface from damage and tarnish. Copper is an efficient heat conductor, but it is a soft material, easily dented and scratched.

LEFT Manufacturers will recommend pots and pans that work most efficiently with their heat source. This type of range also has a special mesh disc (hanging on the right) for toasting bread on the top boiling plate.

RIGHT, CLOCKWISE FROM TOP LEFT This selection of stainless-steel pans and lids is mounted on hooks fixed to a rustic wooden board, accessible to the hob below. Oven gloves are to hand as well.

It's useful to have a variety of sizes and types of pots and pans to suit different needs, from boiling stock and making jam to poaching or frying.

Enamelware has been popular for centuries; the smooth sometimes colourful shiny finish makes it easy to use and clean, and you can choose colours to suit your style.

Utensils & Gadgets So often

we are tempted by the latest and greatest gadget that a manufacturer has created, only to find that the original or older version does the job just as well and doesn't have so many fiddly bits to clean.

ABOVE Find the right utensil for the job and, just as importantly, one that suits the size and shape of your hand so is comfortable to use.

ABOVE RIGHT Favourite baking equipment can be passed on from generation to generation — items that are decades old still do the job well.

Sometimes we buy a special gadget to make a specific recipe. For example, I acquired a cherry stoner when I first made clafoutis, but the stoner has proved useful for pipping black olives and other fruits, too. It is a basic and simple manual gadget that works, rather than a complex electrical machine, and often the simpler the utensil or gadget the less expensive it will be.

There are fashions and phases in this type of kitchen equipment. Slow cookers and pressure cookers have been out of fashion, but are staging a comeback. The pressure cooker dates from the late 1600s, when French physicist Denis Papin, better known for his studies on steam, invented an airtight cooker that used steam pressure to raise the water's boiling point, thus resulting in much quicker cooking. The traditional Italian stovetop Moka coffee maker is another tried and tested machine, invented in the 1930s but still holding its own against the modern pod coffee machines.

OVERLEAF Wooden spatulas and spoons are a staple of any kitchen. They are inexpensive and can easily be replaced if they become tainted, stained or singed.

THIS PAGE Your choice of equipment may be limited by the amount of space you have; if worktop space is scarce then vintage shop scales will be a striking feature but take up valuable room, whereas a modern compact version will fit in a drawer.

THIS PAGE By allocating everything in your kitchen to its own space you will be able to find an item, use and return it ... even if others can't.

Spoons, knives & cutlery

As I mentioned at the beginning of this book some of my best-loved and most useful gadgets and utensils are hand-me-downs and others I have had for years – they are often the classic or original style rather than a new-fangled version.

You can't get much more basic than the wooden spoon. You probably need a couple plus a spatula to get you going, but buy these new – they are inexpensive and in time the wood becomes stained and may absorb pungent flavours such as curry or garlic. A good ladle and a slotted spoon are essential, and although there are many contemporary, moulded plastic and Teflon versions the classic stainless-steel or stove-enamelled types are still around in good cook shops.

A selection of good sharp knives will be at the heart of any kitchen, and although these can be handed down there is a superstition that says you should give someone a coin when they give you a knife. It is believed that this will prevent the knife from cutting the owner, and also that the knife does not cut the friendship between the giver and the recipient.

Stainless-steel knives last well, but some of the older untreated blades will need to be thoroughly dried after use to prevent them from rusting, and will require sharpening from time to time. It is easy to accumulate gadgets and utensils so try, at least once a year, to have a look around your kitchen and dispose of things that you don't use.

FAR LEFT A wall-mounted magnetic knife rack is a safe and easy way to store a variety of sharp utensils.

LEFT Glass jam jars make good cutlery containers and can be run through a dishwasher cycle to keep them sparkling and clean.

BELOW By keeping a utensils jug near a heat source you will allow damp wooden spoons and spurtles to dry out thoroughly.

RIGHT Keep your favourite and most often used gadgets close to where they will be employed – in the long run it saves time.

THIS PAGE Have a variety of chopping boards to suit different tasks, from cutting bread to slicing salamis. These unusual boards with handles could also be used for transporting small tapas-style dishes.

Chopping boards

Although old wooden chopping boards are traditional and attractive, for reasons of hygiene it is best to reserve them for presenting dishes or slicing bread and to have a number of separate, colour-coded polyethylene or glass boards for food preparation.

Wooden boards are made from a number of timbers, such as non-endangered North American hardwoods birch and maple, and beech and olive wood are also popular. Natural wood-fibre composites are less expensive than solid wood and are said not to harbour bacteria. They are also durable, heat-resistant and dishwasher-safe, as are bamboo boards, which have a naturally hygienic quality.

Marble slabs and boards are good for meat preparation because they can be thoroughly cleaned with detergent and boiling water and it is said that pastry is best prepared and rolled on a cool marble surface.

ABOVE RIGHT A wooden pestle and mortar is useful for breaking and blending oily seeds and pods and the softer berries used in making tapenades and pastes.

ABOVE FAR RIGHT Ceramic and stone pestles and mortars are ideal for grinding harder nuts and spices.

RIGHT Pestles and mortars come as a pair so that the tip of the pestle suits the shape and resilience of the bowl.

Pestles & mortars

The mortar is the solid, stout bowl in to which the club-like pestle is pummelled and stirred to grind and crush whatever ingredient is placed into the bowl. These utensils date from the Roman period, when they were used to crush and grind drugs and herbs for medicinal use and they can still be seen in old apothecary or pharmacy signs and labels.

Wood, ceramic, stone, marble and bronze are all used for making culinary pestles and mortars, but the material may dictate what spices or ingredients are prepared within. For example, to make a paste with garlic and ginger you would be better to use a stone or marble combination because the pungent oils and flavours will not impregnate the bowl or pestle point as they would in a set made of unsealed wood. A ceramic bowl and pestle might crack or chip if used to crush a hard shell or kernel while a bronze one would be more than resilient enough to cope with the task.

Kettles & scales

Advances in technolgy mean that kettles can be transparent and illuminated with LED lights so you can watch the bubbles boil, and weighing scales have digital read outs that are accurate to within a milligram. But somehow there is nothing more friendly and reassuring that the timely alert of a whistling kettle on a stove or the moments spent balancing flour or sugar against a manual weight. Vintage pieces are handsome and interesting, so you want to leave them out on show, whereas their modern equivalents are not nearly so appealing to the eye.

ABOVE Old utensils are fine to use in sturdy cast-iron pans, but for those with modern non-stick finishes softer slices and spatulas are less likely to scratch or damage the surface.

RIGHT, CLOCKWISE FROM TOP LEFT Although an electric kettle probably boils more quickly, these classic fluted stovetop versions still have appeal.

An early electric mixer and a vintage shop weighing scales add a touch of nostalgia but are still in working order.

This style of scales was found in traditional grocery stores, and used to weigh loose dried goods, sweets or cheeses and cooked meats.

Traditional weighing scales come with small individual weights. If scales are calibrated to the wrong weight system you can still use the dish as a fruit bowl or platter.

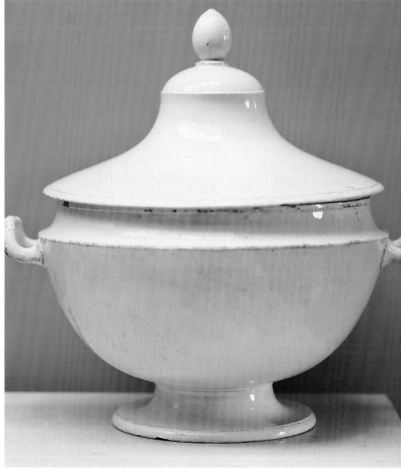

Bowls & jugs

Bowl and jugs come in a wide variety of sizes and materials; they are also essential to any kitchen. You can follow the history and development of mankind through the evolution of these vessels, from the primitive bone, stone or wood dish through to the elaborately painted, fluted and gilded designs of the high Victorian era.

By definition, a bowl or basin is a 'hemispherical vessel, wider than it is deep, used for holding food or fluids', yet they can be as flat as a flan dish or as deep as a soup tureen. The jug, with its tapered, flaring spout and handle, also comes in a wide range of possibilities, although the size is usually linked to the quantity of a liquid it is expected to hold or transport.

For example, among the smallest is the creamer, a petite decorative jug often fashioned in the shape of a cow. It holds pouring cream that is served in small quantities at the table, whereas a milk jug destined to contain milk for a family breakfast table, where bowls of porridge or cereal would be eaten, would be more capacious and utilitarian.

ABOVE LEFT Ceramic mixing bowls are found world wide, and can be used for food preparation and baking as well as storage.

ABOVE This elegant and classically styled soup tureen can be employed to contain and transport soup or cooked vegetables, but may also double as a flower bowl.

A simple white glaze will seal the porous surface of a pottery bowl and make it watertight.

THIS PAGE The humble bowl is a household essential that can be used to serve at every meal from breakfast cereal and lunchtime soup to evening dessert. This simple, stackable style is ideal.

The materials used to make jugs and bowls will also reflect their use and status. Pottery, which includes earthenware, stoneware and porcelain, is widely used. Simple peasant bowls were made from local clay and often glazed to give them a watertight finish otherwise the liquid would be absorbed into the porous fired clay. The glaze also means that they can be hygienically washed in hot water and stored or stacked without the edges being chipped.

At the other end of the scale is fine or bone china, made from kaolin-rich clay fired in a kiln to around 1,200°C (2,192°F), giving toughness, strength and translucency to the china. This type of ware is often referred to as porcelain, which takes its name from the Italian word *porcellana*, which means cowrie shell because of the similarity to the shell's smooth shiny surface.

Glass is also used to make fine glass bowls and jugs, decanters and other table- and storage ware. Glass has the advantage of being transparent, which means the contents can be easily seen, as well as lightweight and versatile, but it is also fragile and delicate. Forms of more toughened glass, such as Pyrex, invented in 1915, have a light and delicate appearance but are oven, microwave and dishwasher proof.

Wood is often used for salad bowls; it should not be washed with detergent but wiped clean and reoiled to preserve the wood. If frequently washed in boiling water with soap the wood may dry and split.

ABOVE FAR LEFT Elegant glassware is a worthwhile addition to any table, but for long-term wine or fortified wine storage you need to ensure that the stopper is a secure and tight fit.

BELOW FAR LEFT Platters and stands once used to display comestibles in a grocery store can be reused as serving plates and containers.

ABOVE LEFT Pudding bowls may be used for mixing small amounts of raw ingredients or as containers for steamed and boiled desserts. With time and use their glaze becomes crackled and pearlized.

LEFT Antique pieces of glassware and pottery may be better admired than used. There will come a time when you feel that their useful days are over and they are best kept out of harm's way.

EVERYDAY TOOLS

✦ Ensure that you use the right utensil for your pots. Many non-stick and Teflon-style finishes will be scratched and damaged if used in conjunction with a metal utensil; a plastic or wooden one will have a softer edge.

✦ Plastic and wooden utensils need to be regularly replaced because strong flavours and the colouring of spices such as turmeric will stain and taint them, and may pass on the absorbed ingredients to subtly flavoured and delicate dishes.

✦ Keep frequently used utensils and gadgets close to the area where you use them. Either hang them from a wall rack or arrange them in a jar or container. But sharp knives are best stored in a block so that the blades are protected from being chipped by other metal objects and your hands are not vulnerable when you select one to use.

✦ Old utensils and gadgets made before the widespread use of stainless steel and metal coatings will be prone to rust unless thoroughly dried, and in some cases dressed with a little oil. The best way to thoroughly dry a metal sieve, cake tin or colander is to put it in the still-warm oven, and leave until the oven is cold and the dish or gadget is completely dry.

LEFT Vintage cream-and-green enamel-coated pots, pans and steamers can still be found in good condition in second-hand shops and car boot sales.

BELOW LEFT A vintage rotary hand whisk, also known as beaters, and a classic Mason Cash glazed stoneware mixing bowl, made by a pottery whose wares date back to the early nineteenth century.

RIGHT, CLOCKWISE FROM TOP LEFT Utensils with hooked handles can be hung on a wall-mounted rail at the front of a stove.

Established in 1920, the Falcon enamelware company is still making its classic pie and bakeware sets, which come in a nest of sizes.

Old French linens are often embroidered with the monogram of the bride for whose trousseau they were made.

An old ceramic pot or jug makes a useful store for spoons, whisks, peelers and the like, but do be sure to give it a wash every now and then to keep grease and crumbs from accumulating in the base.

This colourful enamel Lotus pattern Cathrineholm kettle is believed to have been designed by Arne Clausen in the early 1960s.

Containers

Kitchens are a hub of activity — not just the place where food is stored and prepared, but also where you may feed your family and friends. Each of these activities comes with a set of ingredients and paraphernalia, all of which has to be stored.

Good storage should make it easy to identify the contents. It is time consuming to have to open three identical canisters to see which one holds the sugar when a clear label or a transparent container would have let you do the job in a second.

Size-appropriate containers are also advisable, not just in proportion to the shelf or unit in which they will be kept but also to the contents. It is a waste of space to keep a tablespoon of cloves in a sizable Kilner jar when a small pot would do; also large amounts of air in the jar may cause the contents to deteriorate.

Baskets and bags of all shapes and sizes are versatile containers. Net or string bags and shopping-style baskets can be hung from hooks and used to store vegetables and fruits. Their open structure will allow air to circulate freely, preventing damp and mould. Old crates and wine boxes can also be made into useful storage and double as drawers on open shelves.

LEFT A simple paper doily has been used as a decorative label on recycled jam jars. The label can be easily removed and replaced if the contents are changed.

RIGHT Cooking and baking ware has been made in England by Tala, previously Taylor and Law, since 1899. Their classic 1950s cook's measure (centre top shelf) is still a bestseller.

THIS PAGE Baskets are great for disguising and containing less attractive objects. If they become soiled wipe thoroughly with a wet cloth and allow to dry in the sun or an airing cupboard.

Baskets, boxes & crates

The basket is one of the oldest globally found containers. Most countries have their own style and pattern of basket weaving using a pliable plant that is local to their region, so your basket collection can be made up of vintage, new and exotica picked up on your travels.

Baskets come in all shapes and sizes and can be woven from materials such as jute, rattan and even bamboo, but the sturdiest tend to be made from willow. Companies such as PH Coate & Son have been making willow or withy baskets on the Somerset Levels in England since 1819. They continue to use the same techniques to make a wide range of containers, including the traditional baker's basket, with integral finger holes that make it easier to carry.

Old-fashioned picnic hampers and tray baskets are also worth looking out for, as they come in lots of intereting shapes and designs. They can be lined with a simple cotton cover to protect delicate goods from any rough edges and the cover can also be removed and washed, keeping the basket clean and fresh.

Wooden boxes and crates can be recycled from previous uses; many have been replaced by lightweight and cheaply produced plastic versions so the old soda and apple crates are now used

ABOVE RIGHT An old bottle crate, once used for transporting bottles from the brewery to a shop, still makes a useful container. It could also be used for empty glassware destined for recycling.

RIGHT Industrial-style storage crates are widely available; these metal ones have holes that allow air to circulate around the contents and prevent rust or mould.

as decorative storage. Wooden wine boxes tend to be made of lighter wood than crates and are smaller in size, most big enough to contain six or a dozen bottles. It is fun to find these boxes with their original labels or stamps, often describing the original contents and the manufacturer or distributor who sold them.

As well as wooden wine crates you may also come across metal bottle crates. These might previously have held milk or beer bottles, but nowadays they make a handy recycling container. Rather than fill up valuable bin space with bottles they can be stored in a metal crate or subdivided box then taken to the bottle bank.

These vintage or vintage-style containers make attractive storage that can be arranged on shelves or lined up along the floor, but there is another category of box and crate that is useful but not very pretty. Where the open weave and mesh fabrication of traditional baskets and crates can be an advantage in allowing air to circulate, there are certain things that are best stored in airtight containers, especially if they are to be kept in a cool or damp utility room or pantry, and for these situations a modern opaque plastic crate with a tight-fitting lid is best, but it should be kept out of sight in a cupboard or behind a curtain.

CLOCKWISE FROM FAR LEFT A commercial subdivided wooden tray makes an ideal storage box for glasses — each is kept separate and contained, which will prevent the rims from being chipped.

A raffia cutlery box allows different types of tableware to be kept in individual niches, which also makes table laying a quicker and easier task.

These storage baskets have detachable cotton linings, which prevent small or spiky items from being lost or stuck in the basket's open, woven construction.

Old wooden boxes fitted with matching metal handles have been used as drawers and the area beneath accommodates two deep baskets that are ideal for holding paper or cardboard for recycling.

Glass

Glass containers are a boon in any kitchen because you can see and identify the contents quickly, and also check whether they need to be topped up or replenished. But if the jars and bottles are to be left on show the contents need to be appealing and the containers shiny and clean.

Vintage sweet jars, that once held quantities of humbugs and lemon sherbets, can now be used for storing dried pasta, baking flour and breakfast cereals. Kilner and fruit-preserving jars and bottles are also handy for dried goods that are best kept airtight. If the rubber seals on this type of container start to perish or get damaged it is easy to replace them – either look online or go to a baking shop or hardware store.

You can also recycle jars from current purchases and everyday goods. Some, such as the French brand Bonne Maman, which has an attractive red-and-white gingham-print lid and a faceted jar, make a pleasing display when several are lined up in a row. To recycle a new jar start by soaking it well in warm soapy water to remove the labels. Stubborn patches of glue may need to be eased off with an application of white spirit.

To sterilize the jars pour a kettle of boiling water over them and their lids. When cool enough to handle pour out the water and dry thoroughly in a tepid to warm oven. Then you can make your own labels, not only identifying the contents but maybe using a colour or motif that ties in with your kitchen scheme.

Don't keep a glass jar or container if it becomes cracked or chipped. If it is of particular sentimental value, or especially pretty, you could keep it on display but take it out of regular use to avoid cutting yourself, and before the container breaks and spills its contents. The good thing about standard glassware is that it is relatively inexpensive and easy to replace.

ABOVE FAR LEFT Storage jars can be bought for a specific purpose or fashioned from recycled jam jars, but to be effective they need an efficient airtight seal.

ABOVE LEFT This purpose-made storage system has jug-like containers that slip easily in and out of the shelves. They are not airtight so are best for packets.

ABOVE Glass containers allow you to see and identify the contents without removing the lid, but for some comestibles such as salt and sugar an additional label is useful.

Metal containers

Vintage bread bins and canisters were often enamelled or painted in period colours such as the green and cream of 1950s utility ware, or in the brighter combination of red and white. Because of the difficulty in identifying the contents the tins were labelled with painted panels or pre-printed sticky labels.

Tins were often recycled from branded cereals or hot drinks such as cocoa. When the tin had an attractive brand label, such as the kilted shot putter on Scott's Porridge Oats, or an elegant lady drinking hot chocolate on a brand of drinking chocolate, the tin itself became a prized object and they are now much sought after, and often reproduced. Another form of tin container that was often well decorated and finished was the tea caddy. In the days before the tea bag, loose tea would be measured out in the shop and brought home in a paper bag. The contents of the bag would then be decanted into the caddy and it would have pride of place on the shelf next to the tea pot.

Enamel- and tinware is best for storing dried goods such as tea, grains and cereal. Avoid moist or wet products because they will cause the tin to rust, and these containers are not designed to be watertight.

You could make your own matching set of containers by painting the outside of a number of same-sized tins in a matching shade of paint. There are special enamel paints, such as those used for decorating toy soldiers and model planes, which dry to a hard glossy finish. You could also use household gloss paint, but check the label to ensure that the paints have no toxic ingredients, and allow the tin to dry and air thoroughly, so that the smell of paint has completely gone before you put anything inside.

ABOVE LEFT An enamel bread bin will protect loaves and buns from the drying effect of direct sunlight and when kept in a cool, dry place will also help keep the contents fresh.

LEFT Enamelled containers are popular in many countries and the contents may be indicated in the language of their country of origin.

RIGHT Stainless steel, aluminium and pewter are all metals used to make containers, although contemporary pewter is finished with a lacquer to prevent it from contaminating the contents.

SMALL STORAGE

❧ Spice racks are a great way of containing and displaying a large number of small bottles or jars. The racks are generally narrow so can be fitted on the inside of a unit door or even on the exterior end panel of a cupboard.

❧ Store dull but useful containers inside a larger, more attractive one. Freezer-safe and microwaveable boxes are not usually pretty enough to leave on show, and others that hold mundane products such as washing powder or cleaning solutions tend to be sturdy and utilitarian rather than attractive. By putting them inside another container, such as a close-woven basket or colourful plastic crate, they will be to hand but unseen.

❧ Identify and mark the contents of a plastic container on the lid or side with a non-indelible felt pen. The writing can easily be wiped off and rewritten when the contents are changed and it will be less troublesome than trying to peel off a sticky label.

❧ Subdivide larger containers for more efficient and effective use and choose storage that is specific to a task. For example, a cutlery drawer can be broken down into small sections to separately hold forks, spoons, knives and teaspoons so that they are easy to find and remove.

LEFT Preserving jars, like this rubber-sealed Kilner jar produced by John Kilner & Co in Yorkshire, England, for more than 150 years, can be used to contain dry goods as well as pickles and jams.

RIGHT, CLOCKWISE FROM TOP LEFT These wall-hung enamel salt pots are popular throughout Europe and often come with a small bone or wooden spoon.

Unglazed terracotta pots can be soaked so that they retain water, which makes them useful as wine coolers and places to store fresh herbs.

Colourful storage can brighten up an otherwise plainly decorated kitchen or pantry.

Choose your size of container to suit the contents, putting small quantities of expensive herbs and spices in compact containers and bulkier ingredients such as lentils and rice in bigger jars.

A set of manufactured storage canisters comes with its own purpose-designed shelf system

Suppliers

Shops

Anthropologie
www.anthropologie.com
www.anthropologie.eu
Tel 00800 0026 8476

Augustus Brandt Antiques
Newlands House, Pound Street, Petworth, West Sussex, GU28 0DX
Tel 01798 344722
www.augustus-brandt-antiques.co.uk
Stocks beautiful antiques and also creates contemporary reinterpretations of classic antique furniture.

Crate and Barrel
www.crateandbarrel.com
Kitchen equipment and tableware.

Divertimenti
227–229 Brompton Road, London SW3 2EP
Tel 020 7581 8065
www.divertimenti.co.uk

Fired Earth
Tel 01295 812088
www.firedearth.com
175 Kingswood, Toronto, ON M4E 3N4, Canada
Tel +1 416-686-2399
www.firedearth.ca
Limestone, slate, ceramic, terracotta, sandstone, mosaic and encaustic tiles, plus kitchens and furniture.

Habitat
Tel 0845 601 0740
www.habitat.co.uk
Wide range of contemporary cabinets, furniture and lighting.

House of Hackney
131–132 Shoreditch High Street, London E1 6JE
Tel 020 7739 3257
www.houseofhackney.com
See website for Australian stockists
For fabrics, china and wallpaper.

John Lewis
www.johnlewis.com
Vintage-style kitchenware range.

Labour and Wait
85 Redchurch Street, London E2 7DJ
Tel 020 7729 6253
www.labourandwait.co.uk

Mini Moderns
Tel 020 7737 6767
www.minimoderns.com
For wallpaper, kitchen textiles and china.

Objects of Use
6 Lincoln House, Market Street, Oxford OX1 3EQ
Tel 01865 241705
www.objectsofuse.com
Great range of cook, clean and house products.

Possessed N1
96 Chapel Street Market, London N1 9EY
To make an appointment please contact tania@possessedn1.com
Tel 020 7278 0901
www.possessedn1.com
Glamour, individuality and style with a constantly changing stock of furniture, fabrics and tableware.

RE
Bishops Yard, Main Street, Corbridge, Northumberland, NE45 5LA
Tel 01434 634567
www.re-foundobjects.com
For rare and remarkable, recycled, rescued and restored goods as well as originals and textiles designed by RE.

Summerill & Bishop
100 Portland Road, London, W11 4LQ
Tel 020 7221 4566
www.summerillandbishop.com
Stock a wide range of kitchen, dining and tableware.

Sur La Table
www.surlatable.com
Kitchen accessories and bakeware.

Williams Sonoma
www.williams-sonomainc.com
All styles of kitchen equipment and tableware.

Flooring

Amtico
www.amtico.com
Producing some of the most inspirational flooring designs for nearly 50 years.

Harvey Maria
Tel 0845 680 1231
www.harveymaria.co.uk
Vinyl flooring that is tough, durable, scuff and scratch resistant and easy to clean. Includes designs by Cath Kidston and Neisha Crosland.

Rustica
154c Milton Park, Abingdon, OX14 4SA
Tel 01235 834192
Terracotta tiles.

Lighting

Anglepoise
Anglepoise.com
Classic work lights.

BTC Lighting
288 Chelsea Harbour, The Design Centre, London SW10 0XE
Tel 01993 882251
www.originalbtc.com
Original and classic designs.

Rockett St George
www.rockettstgeorge.co.uk

Furniture & Kitchens

The Conran Shop
Michelin House, 81 Fulham Road, London SW3
Tel 020 7589 7401
www.conran.co.uk
Contemporary and ethnic cupboards; also good for seating and tableware.

Ercol
Summerleys Road, Princes Risborough, Bucks HP27 9PX
Tel 01844 271 800
www.ercol.com
www.ercol.com.au
Furniture makers since 1920, many classic designs still in production. Available through 150 independent furniture stores across the UK. Also exclusive ranges at John Lewis, The White Company and Feather & Black.

Heal's
196 Tottenham Court Road London W1T 7LQ
www.heals.co.uk
Contemporary and retro-style kitchenware.

Martin Moore & Company
Tel 0845 180 0015
www.martinmoore.com
Produce handmade kitchens of the highest quality and craftsmanship. Design and fitting service throughout the UK.

Plain English
www.plainenglishdesign.co.uk

China & Kitchenware

Le Creuset
www.lecreuset.com
www.lecreuset.ca
www.lecreuset.com.au
Cast-iron and enamel premium cookware, kitchenware, bakeware and wine accessories.

Falcon Enamelware
www.falconenamelware.com

Falk Culinair
www.falkculinair.com
www.falkcoppercookware.ca
www.copperkitchen.com.au
Specializes in the manufacturing of professional-grade copper cookware of outstanding quality.

Loaf
www.loaf.com

Mason Cash
www.masoncash.co.uk
Classic biscuit-coloured mixing bowls with white interiors. Available through Lakeland and department stores.

Mauviel
Mauviel USA, Inc.
802 Centerpoint Blvd. New Castle, DE 19720
Tel (302) 326-4803
www.mauvielusa.com
mauvielcanada.com
Cookware manufactured in copper, stainless steel and aluminium.

Orla Kiely
www.orlakiely.com
For retro-inspired kitchenware.

Pyrex
www.arc-international-cookware.com
A leading brand of cookware historically known for its heat-resistant glass range that covers prepware, bakeware, ovenware and storage items. Widely available through cook shops and department stores including Walmart.

Riess Kitchenware
www.riesskitchenware.com
Enamelware.

Tala by Taylor & Law
www.talacooking.com
Baking, preserving and icing wares.

Utility Design
www.utilitydesign.co.uk
Utility ware.

Wedgwood
www.wedgwood.co.uk
waterfordwedgwood.ca
www.wwrd.com.au/wedgwood/
Classic English china since 1759, from plain to pretty and ornate designs. Widely available through department stores and specialist china shops.

Wheel and Barrow
www.wheelandbarrow.com.au
Mail order kitchenware, cookware and bakeware.

Storage

PH Coate & Son
Meare Green Court, Stoke St Gregory, Taunton, Somerset TA3 6HY
Tel 01823 490249
www.englishwillowbaskets.co.uk
A wide range of willow baskets, boxes and storage containers.

Index

Acknowledgements

Photographic credits

1 Penny Duncan's kitchen, London / Jacqui Small LLP, Andrew Wood; 2 © living4media / Ira Leoni; 3 William Waldron / The Interior Archive; 4 www.jamesbalston.com (antiques dealer Paula Parkinson's home, Normandy); 5 © living4media / Winfried Heinze; 5 © living4media / Winfried Heinze; 6 and 7 Possessed N1 / Jacqui Small LLP, Darren Chung; 8 left Tony Baratta's house in Long Island / Jacqui Small LLP, Andrew Wood; 8 right Dominique Kieffer's house in Normandy / Jacqui Small LLP, Simon Upton; 9 Polly Eltes / Narratives; 10 © living4media / Evangelos Paterakis; 11 Adrian Sherratt / Alamy; 12 below left © living4media / The Interior Archive / Simon Upton; 12 above left and above right Possessed N1 / Jacqui Small LLP, Darren Chung; 12 below right Hans Zeegers / taverne-agency.com; 13 left Matthew Williams/ taverne-agency.com; 13 right Chris Bortugno's house in upstate New York / Jacqui Small LLP, Simon Upton; 14 David Parmiter / Narratives; 16–27 Martin Moore & Co / Jacqui Small LLP, Darren Chung; 28 Andreas von Einsiedel; 31 Nathalie Krag / Mauro & Giovanna / taverne-agency.com; 32 above and below Tony Baratta's house in Long Island / Jacqui Small LLP, Andrew Wood; 33 Tony Baratta's house in Long Island / Jacqui Small LLP, Andrew Wood; 34 and 35 www.jamesbalston.com; 36 and 37 Bernd Opitz / Arthurs Circus / taverne-agency.com; 38 Ngoc Minh Ngo / Holzman / taverne-agency.com; 39 Nathalie Krag/ Luca and Silvia / taverne-agency.com; 40 left © living4media / Winfried Heinze; 40 right © Tom Leighton / Livingetc/ IPC+ Syndication; 41 © living4media / EWAStock; 42 Micky Hoyle / Livingetc / IPC+ Syndication; 43 Camera Press / Zuhause Wohne; 44 GAP Interiors / Dan Duchar; 45 Darren Chung / The kitchen of the artists Freddie Robins & Ben Coode-Adams. Design & build: Ben Coode-Adams, Hudson Architects, Nick Spall (NS Restorations) and Nicol Wilson; 46 and 47 Designed by Solis Betancourt, The Hamptons

/ Jacqui Small LLP, Andrew Wood; 48 left and right Andreas von Einsiedel/ Kenyon Kramer & Jean Louis Raynaud; 49 www.jamesbalston.com; Trolley designed and made by John Plowman shown in the kitchen of artist Nicola Streeten <nicolastreeten@yahoo.com>; 50 and 51 Nicolas Mathéus/ The Interior Archive, Stylist: Laurence Dougier, Architect: Katerina Tsigarida; 52 Dos Santos Solvi / hemis.fr / hometica.com; 53 Rachel Whiting / GAP / hometica.com; 54 Nicolas Mathéus / Côté Paris / The Interior Archive, Stylist: Laurence Dougier, Designer: Emmanuel Dougier; 56 Nicolas Matheus / Côté Sud / The Interior Archive, Stylist: Laurence Dougier, Designer: Josephine Ryan; 57 Mr and Mrs Sagbakken's cabin (Norway) interior design by Helence Forbes-Hennie / Jacqui Small LLP, Simon Upton; 58 and 59 Kristiina Ratia's House, Connecticut / Jacqui Small LLP, Andrew Wood; 60 and 61 Andreas von Einsiedel / Fiona Adamczeswki; 62 left Andreas von Einsiedel/ Mark Hix; 62 right © living4media / ISTL; 63 © living4media / The Interior Archive / Simon Upton / Designer/ Stylist: Sharon Simonaire; 64 left Sophie Munro / Red Cover / hometica.com; 64 right © living4media / Björnsdotter, Magdalena; 65 Plain English; 66 above Andreas von Einsiedel / Holger Stewen; 66 below Andreas von Einsiedel / Fiona Adamczeswki; 67 © living4media / Lars Ranek; 68 Photoshot / Red Cover / Evan Sklar; 69 above Mikkel Vang / taverne-agency.com; 69 below Polly Eltes / Narratives; 70 background Radius Images / Alamy; 70 above © living4media / View Pictures; 70 below James Fennell / The Interior Archive; 71 © living4media / The Interior Archive / Simon Upton / Designer/ Stylist: Ilaria Miani; 72 left © living4media / EWAStock; 72 right © living4media / Annette & Christian; 73 Anouk de Kleermaeker / Heleen and Marnix / taverne-agency.com; 74 © living4media / Magdalena Björnsdotter; 75 left Wauman Luc / hemis.fr/ hometica.com; 75 right Andreas von Einsiedel / Alison Sloga; 76 left Dos Santos Solvi / hemis.fr / hometica.com; 76 above right

Robbert Koene / Churchaven / taverne-agency.com; 76 below right © living4media / The Interior Archive / Kordakis, Yiorgos; 77 © living4media / Lars Ranek; 78 background Getty Images/ Tetra images RF; 78 above Jean-Marc Palisse / Côté Est, Stylist: Alix de Dives; 78 below © living4media / Brando Cimarosti; 79 Anthony Collett's house in Tuscany / Jacqui Small LLP, Simon Upton; 80 Andreas von Einsiedel / Peter Nolden; 81 © living4media / Christophe Madamour; 82 © living4media / The Interior Archive / Stefano Scata / Designer/ Stylist: Silvio Stefani; 83 Christopher Simon Sykes / The Interior Archive; 84 Andreas von Einsiedel / Lachlan Stewart; 84 Andreas von Einsiedel / Lachlan Stewart; 85 © living4media / The Interior Archive / Simon Upton / Designer/ Stylist: Peter Marston; 86 Glen Senk & Keith Johnson's house, Philidelphia / Jacqui Small LLP, Simon Upton; 87 © living4media / The Interior Archive / Fritz von der Schulenburg; 88 Marc van Praag / The Interior Archive, Designer: Beatrix Kleuver; 89 Fritz & Dana Rohn's Connecticut house / Jacqui Small LLP, Simon Upton; 90 background Andreas von Einsiedel / Gioconda Cicogna; 90 Andreas von Einsiedel / Debbie Bliss; 91 William Yeoward's house in the country / Jacqui Small LLP, Simon Upton; 92 © living4media / EWAStock; 93 Andreas von Einsiedel / Susanne Bisovski; 94 left Possessed N1 / Jacqui Small LLP, Darren Chung 94 right Andreas von Einsiedel / Sue Timney; 95 Matthew Williams / Pittstown House / taverne-agency.com; 96 © living4media / Geertsen, Luuk; 97 Emma Hawkins House, Edinburgh / Jacqui Small LLP, Simon Upton 98 and 99 Lena Proudlock of Denim Instyle's house in Gloucestershire / Jacqui Small LLP, Simon Upton; 100 left Anthony Cochrane's apartment, New York / Jacqui Small LLP, Simon Upton; 100 right Ali Sharlands house, Gloucester / Jacqui Small LLP, Simon Upton; 101 Ann Mollo's House, London /Jacqui Small LLP, Simon Upton; 102 ©living4media / StockFood / Tanya Zouev; 103 Glen Senk and Keith Johnson's house, Philidelphia / Jacqui Small LLP,

Simon Upton; 104 background Getty Images; 104 above © living4media / The Interior Archive / Bob Smith; 105 Wauman Luc / hemis.fr / hometica.com; 106 Mikkel Vang / taverne-agency.com; 107 Mikkel Vang / taverne-agency.com; 108 © living4media / The Interior Archive / Simon Upton, Designer/ Stylist: Will Fisher/ Jamb; 109 Photoshot / Red Cover / Paul Massey; 110 and 111 Andreas von Einsiedel / Paola Navone; 112 left Snow kitchen table with Café au Lait chairs / available from Loaf.com; 112 right Jean Louis Raynaud and Kenyon Kraymer's house, Provence / Jacqui Small LLP, Simon Upton; 113 Zinc kitchen table with Geronimo and Café au Lait chairs / available from Loaf.com; 114 Alex Van de Walles Apartment, Brussels / Jacqui Small LLP, Simon Upton; 115 Peter and Marijke de Wit of Domaine d' Heerstaagen, Netherlands / Jacqui Small LLP, Simon Upton; 116 Josephine Ryan's house in London / Jacqui Small LLP, Simon Upton; 117 © living4media / Bertrand Limbour; 118 © living4media / Interior Archive / Bill Batten / Designer/ Stylist: Lim Conner & Jake Opperman; 119 left Mikkel Vang / taverne-agency.com; 119 right Andreas von Einsiedel / John Chapman; 120 Andreas von Einsiedel / Bruno & Alexandre Lafourcade; 121 © living4media / Taverne Agency b.v. / Dana van Leeuwen; 122 Possessed N1 / Jacqui Small LLP, Darren Chung 123 left GAP Interiors / Devis Bionaz; 123 right Holly Jolliffe / Narratives; 124 © living4media / Bine Bellmann; 125 top left Possessed N1 / Jacqui Small LLP, Darren Chung 125 below left www.jamesbalston.com ; 125 above right Elisabeth Aarhus / Mainstreamimages / auslortebandepiker.no; 125 below right Brent Darby / Narratives; 126 left Andreas von Einsiedel / Michael Playford; 127 Andreas von Einsiedel / Kate Armitage; 128 left © living4media / Sheltered Images; 128 right © living4media / Taverne Agency b.v. / van Leeuwen, Dana; 129 left © living4media / Gallo Images Pty Ltd.; 129 right Patrick van Robaeys / Côté Ouest, Stylist: Sylvie Lajouanie, Designer: Henk Teunissen; 130 left Eric d'Herouville / Côté

Ouest, Stylist: Marie-Maud Levron; 130 right © living4media / Christine Bauer; 131 GAP Interiors / Ingrid Rasmussen; 132 Tuscany, Italy / Jacqui Small LLP, Simon Upton; 133 Andreas von Einsiedel / James Perkins; 134 above © living4media / The Interior Archive / Simon Upton / Designer/ Stylist: Sharon Simonaire; 134 below © living4media / The Interior Archive / Marc Luscombe-Whyte, Designer/ Stylist: Philippe Brown; 135 Axel Vervoordt's house in Belgium / Jacqui Small LLP, Simon Upton; 136 The Kitchen / Jacqui Small LLP, Andrew Wood / The Interior Archive; 137 William Waldron / The Interior Archive, Stylist: Carlos Mota, Designer: Diego Uchitel; 138 GAP Interior Images Ltd; 139 above left © living4media / The Interior Archive / Fritz von der Schulenburg / Designer/ Stylist: Mimmi O'Connell; 139 above right Brent Darby / Narratives; 139 below Henri del Olmo / Côté Sud, Stylist: Genevieve Dortignac, La Maison de Constance; 140 above GAP Interiors / Douglas Gibb; 140 left EWA Stock / hometica.com; 140 left EWA Stock / hometica.com; 141 © living4media / The Interior Archive / Alex Ramsay / Designer/ Stylist: Dorian Bowen; 142 left © living4media / Misha Vetter; 142 right Possessed N1 / Jacqui Small LLP, Darren Chung William Waldron / The Interior Archive, Designer Keith Johnson; 144 left Nathalie Krag / Mauro & Giovanna / taverne-agency.com; 144 above right www.jamesbalston.com / Armorel Kitchens; 144 below right Andreas von Einsiedel / Dingwall Main; 145 Andreas von Einsiedel / Victoria Hiliard; 146 above Andreas von Einsiedel / Michael Playford; 146 below Ngoc Minh / taverne-agency.com; 147 Dos Santos Solvi / hemis.fr / hometica.com; 148 © living4media / The Interior Archive / Tim Beddow / Designer/ Stylist: Penny Morrison; 149 Andreas von Einsiedel / Hugh Henry; 150 left © living4media / Johnér; 150 right © living4media / Taverne Agency b.v. / Henk Brandsen; 151 Guillaume de Laubier / Côté Ouest, Stylist: Pascale de la Cochetiere; 152

left © living4media / Jo Tyler; **152 right** © living4media / View Pictures; **153 right** Andreas von Einsiedel / Charlotte Crosland; **154** © living4media / Lars Ranek; **155** Andreas von Einsiedel / Andrei Dmitriev; **156** © living4media / Johnér; **157** Anouk de Kleermaeker / Yvonne's Place / taverne-agency.com; **158** © living4media / The Interior Archive / Simon Upton / Designer/ Stylist: Robert Stilin Architect: Frank Greenwald; **159 above left** Narratives; **159 above right** Brent Darby / Narratives; **159 below left** © living4media / Magdalena Björnsdotter; **159 below right** Brent Darby / Narratives; **160** Mikkel Vang / taverne-agency.com **161** www.jamesbalston.com (antiques dealer Paula Parkinson's home in Normandy); **162 left** Andreas von Einsiedel/ Chris Barclay & Michael Voigt; **162 right** Tony Baratta's house, Long Island / Jacqui Small LLP, Andrew Wood; **163 left** Andreas von Einsiedel / Joris van Grinsven; **163 right** Matthew Williams / Inderbitzen / taverne-agency.com; **164 left** Mikkel Vang / taverne-agency.com; **164 right** and **165 right** Designed by Solis Betancourt, The Hamptons / Jacqui Small LLP, Andrew Wood; **165 left** www.jamesbalston.com / Armorel Kitchens; **166** © living4media / Bertrand Limbour; **167 left** Andreas von Einsiedel/ Alvise Orsini; **167 right** Alexander James/ The Interior Archive, Architect: Nagan Johnson; **168 above** GAP Interiors / Rachel Whiting; **168 below** © living4media / Lars Ranek; **169** © living4media / The Interior Archive / Fritz von der Schulenburg / Designer/ Stylist: Mimmi O'Connell; **170 left** Axel Vervoordt's house in

Belgium / Jacqui Small LLP, Simon Upton **170 right** Axel Vervoordt's house in Belgium / Jacqui Small LLP, Simon Upton; **171** Andreas von Einsiedel / Pierredon; **172 above** © living4media / Magdalena Björnsdotter; **172 below left** © living4media / Alexander James; **172 below right** Bernard Touillon / *Côté Sud*, Stylist: Cecile Vavarelli; **173** © living4media / The Interior Archive/ Simon Upton / Designer/ Stylist: Sheila Scholes; **174** Martin Lof/ taverne-agency.com; **175 left** Marjon Hoogervorst / taverne-agency.com; **175 right** Nathalie Krag / Jens / taverne-agency.com; **176** Andreas von Einsiedel / Charlotte Crosland; **177** Carol Egan Interiors www.caroleganinteriors.com/ Richard Powers; **178 left** © living4media / Christine Bauer, **178 right** © living4media / The Interior Archive / Bill Batten / Designer/ Stylist: Lim Conner & Jake Opperman; **179** © living4media / Lars Ranek; **180** © living4media / Vierucci / Eustachi; **181** Nicolas Matheus / The Interior Archive, Stylist: Laurence Dougier, Architect: Sabrina Bignami; **182** © living4media / The Interior Archive/ Frédéric Vasseur; **183** © living4media / Jo Tyler; **184** Anne Dokter / taverne-agency.com; **185 above left** Ray Main / Mainstreamimages / Alistair Hendy Design; **185 above right** Nathalie Krag / taverne-agency.com; **185 below left** Albert Font / *Côté Sud*, Stylist: Genevieve Dortignac; **185 below right** © living4media / Gallo Images Pty Ltd.; **186 left** Jean Louis Raynaud and Kenyon Kraymer's house, Provence / Jacqui Small LLP, Simon Upton **186 right** William Waldron / The Interior Archive, Designer:

Keith Johnson; **187** and **188** Frank Faulkner's house in Upstate New York / Jacqui Small LLP, Simon Upton; **188** © living4media / Nele Braas; **189** Andreas von Einsiedel / Lafourcade; **190** Andreas von Einsiedel / Chateau Rigaud; **191 above left** © living4media / Brando Cimarosti; **191 above right** Andreas von Einsiedel / Gabrielle Tana; **191 below** Getty Images / StockFood; **192 left** Claire Richardson / Narratives; **192 right** Robbert Koene / taverne-agency.com; **193** Mikkel Vang / taverne-agency.com; **194** Andreas von Einsiedel/ Fiona Adamczeswki; **196 left** Andreas von Einsiedel / Stephen Bailey; **196 right** © living4media / Catherine Gratwicke; **197 left** © living4media / Winfried Heinze; **197 right** Gilles Trillard / *Côté Ouest*, Stylist: Marie-Maud Levron; **198** Patrick van Robaeys / *Côté Est*, Stylist: Marine Broussaud, Design: Polyedre; **199 left** www.jamesbalston.com; **199 above right** Andreas von Einsiedel / Samways; **199 below** © living4media / Nele Braas; **200** Possessed N1 / Jacqui Small LLP, Darren Chung **201 above left** © living4media / Winfried Heinze; **201 below right** © living4media / June Tuesday; **202 left** Peri Wolfman & Charles Gold's house, Bridgehampton / Upton, Simon; **203** Josephine Ryan's house, London / Jacqui Small LLP, Simon Upton **204 below** www.jamesbalston.com (antiques dealer Paula Parkinson's home in Normandy); **204 above** and **205** Josephine Ryan's house, London / Jacqui Small LLP, Simon Upton; **206** Possessed N1 / Jacqui Small LLP, Darren Chung **207 above left** © living4media / Winfried Heinze; **207 above right** Possessed N1

/ Jacqui Small LLP, Darren Chung **207 below left** GAP Interiors / Devis Bionaz; **207 centre right** © living4media / Bine Bellmann; **207 below right** © living4media / Winfried Heinze; **208** © living4media / Franziska Taube; **209** GAP Interiors / Colin Poole; **210** © living4media / Lars Ranek; **211 above** and **below** © living4media / Winfried Heinze; **212 left** Andreas von Einsiedel / hometica.com; **212 above right** Andreas von Einsiedel / Bruno & Alexandre Lafourcade; **212 below right** GAP Interiors / Jake Fitzjones; **213** David Parmiter / Narratives; **214 left** Andreas von Einsiedel / Jennifer Lloyd; **214 right** Arcaid Images / Alamy; **216 above** GAP Interiors / Colin Poole; **216 below** GAP Interiors / Colin Poole; **217** © living4media / The Interior Archive / Fritz von der Schulenburg / Designer/ Stylist: Juliette Mole; **218** Radius Image / Alamy; **219 above left** Andreas von Einsiedel / Debbie Urquhart; **219 centre left** GAP Interiors / Bruce Hemming; **219 centre right** GAP Interiors / Maxwell Attenborough; **219 below** www.jamesbalston.com / Armorel Kitchens

Endpapers
All Jacqui Small LLP. All Possessed N1 / Darren Chung apart from:
Front, top row 3 Peri Wolfman and Charles Gold's house, Bridgehampton / Simon Upton; **4** Josephine Ryan's house, London / Simon Upton; **centre row 1** Chris Bortugno's House Upstate New York / Simon Upton; **4** Martin Moore & Co / Darren Chung; **5** Designed by Solis Betancourt, The Hamptons / Andrew Wood; **bottom row 2** Martin Moore & Co / Darren

Chung; **3** Josephine Ryan's house, London / Simon Upton; **4** William Yeoward's house in the country / Simon Upton; **6** Peter and Marijke de Wit of Domaine d' Heerstaagen, Netherlands / Simon Upton; **Back, top row 2** Designed by Solis Betancourt, The Hamptons / Andrew Wood; **3** Martin Moore & Co / Darren Chung **4** Josephine Ryan's house, London / Simon Upton; **6** Josephine Ryan's house, London / Simon Upton; **centre row 1** Tony Baratta's house in Long Island / Andrew Wood; **2** Martin Moore & Co / Darren Chung; **3** Designed by Solis Betancourt, The Hamptons / Andrew Wood; **5** Penny Duncan's Kitchen, London / Andrew Wood; **6** ; Ali Sharland's house, Gloucester / Simon Upton; **top row 1** and **3** Lena Proudlock of Denim Instyle's house in Gloucestershire / Simon Upton; **2** Josephine Ryan's house, London / Simon Upton; **4** Peter and Marijke de Wit of Domaine d' Heerstaagen, Netherlands / Simon Upton; **5** Frank Faulkner's house, upstate New York / Simon Upton; **6** Anthony Cochrane's apartment, New York / Simon Upton

Front Cover www.jamesbalston.com;
Back Cover above right www.jamesbalston.com (antiques dealer Paula Parkinson's home, Normandy);
Back Cover below right Andreas von Einsiedel / Fiona Adamczeswki;
Back Cover left Josephine Ryan's house, London / Jacqui Small LLP, Simon Upton

Author acknowledgements

Special thanks to:

Barbara Moore of Martin Moore & Company, and **Toni Silver** and **Andrew Wartnaby** of the Esher Martin Moore & Company showroom for allowing us to use their English kitchen for our special photography (pages 16–27); also to **Jenny Hildreth** and **Marie Reynolds** of ARC PR for all their help in setting up our days in residence.

Mark Hampshire, Keith Stephenson and **Charlotte Noakes** of Mini Moderns who whirled through like a blue tornado and made a hard day's work such fun.

June Summerill and **Bernadette Bishop** of Summerill & Bishop for their brilliant ideas and deft execution, **Jon Summerill** for his transportation skills and **Lucy Morris** for her packing, unpacking, packing and unpacking.

Frieda Gormley and **Javvy M Royle** of House of Hackney for inspiring an interest in Hackney history and for making the trip after the school run. Also to **Kate Champion** of The Communication Store for all her help in setting up the times and dates.

Tania Rowling of Possessed N1 for the use of her wonderful English Rose kitchen and restorative cups of strong coffee.

Darren Chung for his support, photographic expertise and help in wallpaper hanging.

And the team: **Jacqui Small**, our guiding light; **Jo Copestick**, who manages everything, **Sian Parkhouse**, simply the best editor in town, **Penny Stock** for wonderful design, **Claire Hamilton** for great pictures, **Alexandra Labbe Thompson** for coffee and sustenance during long picture meetings; and **Jessica Axe** who gets people to sit up and notice all the hard work that has been put into making a book.